Learning to Write for Readers

NCTE Editorial Board

Learning to Write for Readers

Using Brain-Based Strategies

John T. Crow

National Council of Teachers of English
1111 W. Kenyon Road, Urbana, Illinois 61801-1096

Manuscript Editor: JAS Group
Staff Editor: Bonny Graham
Interior Design: Jenny Jensen Greenleaf
Cover Design: Pat Mayer
Cover Image: iStockphoto.com / tmietty

NCTE Stock Number: 27827

It is the policy of NCTE in its journals and other publications to provide a forum for the open discussion of ideas concerning the content and the teaching of English and the language arts. Publicity accorded to any particular point of view does not imply endorsement by the Executive Committee, the Board of Directors, or the membership at large, except in announcements of policy, where such endorsement is clearly specified.

Every effort has been made to provide current URLs and email addresses, but because of the rapidly changing nature of the Web, some sites and addresses may no longer be accessible.

Library of Congress Cataloging-in-Publication Data

Crow, John T.
    Learning to write for readers : using brain-based strategies / John T. Crow.
       p. cm.
    Includes bibliographical references.
    ISBN 978-0-8141-2782-7 ((pbk))
    1. English language—Composition and exercises—Study and teaching. 2. Learning—Physiological aspects. I. Title.
    LB1576.C828 2011
    372.62'3044—dc23

                                                                2011029955

Contents

PREFACE xi

CHAPTER 1 Feeding Reading 1

The Proficient Reader 2

EYE MOVEMENT 2

CLASSROOM DEMONSTRATION: EYE MOVEMENT 2

WORD FOR WORD? 3

CLASSROOM DEMONSTRATION: WORD FOR WORD 1 3

CLASSROOM DEMONSTRATION: WORD FOR WORD 2 5

Sample-Predict-Confirm 5

CLASSROOM DEMONSTRATION: ERRONEOUS PREDICTION 5

The GUESS Error 7

CLASSROOM DEMONSTRATION: PROFESSIONAL GUESSING 7

CLASSROOM DEMONSTRATION: STUDENT GUESSING 8

CLASSROOM APPLICATION: GUESS ERRORS 10

CLASSROOM ACTIVITY: ROUND-ROBIN WRITING .13

Reading like Writers 14

CLASSROOM ACTIVITY: RECONSTRUCTING TRANSITIONS 14

CLASSROOM APPLICATION: EXTENDING THE RECONSTRUCTION 17

Summary 18

Further Reading 19

CHAPTER 2 Economy of Effort and the Self-Googling Brain 20

The Self-Googling Brain 20

CLASSROOM DEMONSTRATION: HUMANS VERSUS COMPUTERS

PART IA 21

CLASSROOM DEMONSTRATION: HUMANS VERSUS COMPUTERS
PART IB...22
Schemas and Scripts...23
CLASSROOM DEMONSTRATION: HUMANS VERSUS COMPUTERS
PART II...23
Inferences...25
CLASSROOM ACTIVITY: INFERENCES.....................................25
CLASSROOM ACTIVITY: CHANGING AUDIENCES 26
Self-Googling: A Problem for Writers.................................27
CLASSROOM ACTIVITY: THINKING ABOUT AUDIENCE.......................28
Chunking...28
CLASSROOM DEMONSTRATION: CHUNKING 28
Background Knowledge...31
CLASSROOM DEMONSTRATION: BACKGROUND KNOWLEDGE
AND MEMORY 31
CLASSROOM DEMONSTRATION: OPTICAL ILLUSION 33
Economy of Effort and Writing 37
Summary 39
Further Reading..40

CHAPTER 3   Reader Expectations and the Essay 41
The Power of the Title 41
CLASSROOM DEMONSTRATION: TITLE INSURANCE.........................42
The Role of the Introduction 43
CLASSROOM DEMONSTRATION: THE BAD INTRODUCTION............43
CLASSROOM DEMONSTRATION: THE GOOD INTRODUCTION..........45
CLASSROOM ACTIVITY: GUESS FROM THE INTRODUCTION 46
The Role of a Topic Sentence or Thesis Statement....................46
CLASSROOM DEMONSTRATION: DO WHAT? 47
Transitions 48
CLASSROOM ACTIVITY: RECONSTRUCTIVE SURGERY 49
CLASSROOM ACTIVITY: CREATE A PATIENT 51
Punctuation 52
CLASSROOM DEMONSTRATION: GUESS SIGNALS.....................52
PUNCTUATION SUMMARY...55
Summary 56
Further Reading..57

CHAPTER 4 Reading like Writers 58
Analyzing Texts 59
    CLASSROOM ACTIVITY: MINING TEXTS 60
    CLASSROOM APPLICATION: TEXT-MINING COMPETITION 63
    CLASSROOM APPLICATION: TEXT-MINING LOGS 65
    CLASSROOM ACTIVITY: SAYS–DOES 65
    CLASSROOM ACTIVITY: WRITING LOGS 66
Audience 68
    CLASSROOM ACTIVITY: GUESS THE AUDIENCE 68
    CLASSROOM ACTIVITY: CHANGE THE AUDIENCE 71
    CLASSROOM ACTIVITY: CONTRAST THE AUDIENCE 71
Summary 75
Further Reading 76

CHAPTER 5 Exploring the Concept of Sentence 77
What Is a Sentence? 77
    CLASSROOM DEMONSTRATION: AN INADEQUATE DEFINITION OF
        SENTENCE 78
    CLASSROOM ACTIVITY: FIVE WORDS IN A SENTENCE 80
Sentence Gathering 81
    CLASSROOM ACTIVITY: SENTENCE SPOTLIGHT 81
    CLASSROOM ACTIVITY: NAME THAT SENTENCE 83
Sentences as Building Blocks 86
    CLASSROOM DEMONSTRATION: KNOWN-NEW CONTRACT 86
    CLASSROOM ACTIVITY: TOPIC-COMMENT CONNECTIONS 87
    CLASSROOM APPLICATION: TRACE THE LINKAGE—PROFESSIONAL
        WRITING 90
    CLASSROOM APPLICATION: TRACE THE LINKAGE—STUDENT
        WRITING 91
Summary 92
Further Reading 93

CHAPTER 6 Exploring the Concept of Paragraph 94
Paragraph Definition 94
    CLASSROOM ACTIVITY: AN INADEQUATE DEFINITION OF
        PARAGRAPH 95
Playing with Paragraphs 98
    CLASSROOM ACTIVITY: MULTI-PARAGRAPH TOPIC MAINTENANCE 99
    CLASSROOM APPLICATION: MULTI-PARAGRAPH TOPIC
        MAINTENANCE 102

CLASSROOM ACTIVITY: MINING PARAGRAPHS 103

Scope Creep 104

CLASSROOM ACTIVITY: TWO TYPES OF SCOPE CREEP 105

Summary 107

CHAPTER 7   Exploring the Concept of Essay 109

Essay Parts 109

TITLE PLUS INTRODUCTION 110

CLASSROOM ACTIVITY: MISSING PIECES 110

THE INTRODUCTION 112

THE CONCLUSION 115

THE BODY 116

A Blueprint for Writing 119

The Research Paper Genre 121

THE I-SEARCH PAPER 122

Plagiarism 123

Receptive Knowledge 124

Summary 124

Further Reading 125

CHAPTER 8   Dialectically Diverse Writers 126

Language Awareness 127

INSTRUCTIONS AND SURVEY 127

Closing the Achievement Gap in Writing 134

LABELING AND CODE SWITCHING 134

IN THE CLASSROOM 136

CLASSROOM ACTIVITY: DAMAGE CONTROL 136

CLASSROOM ACTIVITY: FLIP THE SWITCH 137

Contrastive Analysis 139

CONTRASTIVE ANALYSIS FOR TEACHERS 139

CLASSROOM ACTIVITY: CONTRASTIVE ANALYSIS FOR STUDENTS 140

Summary 142

Further Reading 142

APPENDIX A: PARIS IN THE SPRING SIGN 143

APPENDIX B: TEXTUAL ANALYSIS WORKSHEET 144

APPENDIX C: SENTENCE LINKAGE WORKSHEET 145

WORKS CITED..147

INDEX...153

AUTHOR 157

Preface

The Current State of Affairs

Let's face it: too many student writers go from grade to grade to graduation, "forgetting" concepts, skills, and strategies from previous years and showing little improvement in their writing skills. Some of these students receive additional classes in writing at the college level, yet too many of them enter the workplace ill prepared to express themselves properly in writing.

The National Commission on Writing in America's Schools and Colleges issued a report on the status of writing in 2003 titled *The Neglected "R."* The commission noted that "it would be false to claim that most students cannot write. What most students cannot do is write well. At least, they cannot write well enough to meet the demands they face in higher education and the emerging work environment. Basic writing is not the issue; the problem is that most students cannot write with the skill expected of them today" (16).

The following year, this same commission published another report, *Writing: A Ticket to Work . . . Or a Ticket Out*. The commission surveyed 120 major American corporations that employed almost 8 million people. Here are two of the findings:

1. "People who cannot write and communicate clearly will not be hired and are unlikely to last long enough to be considered for promotion." (3)

2. "Based on survey responses, it appears that remedying deficiencies in writing may cost American firms as much as $3.1 billion annually." (4)

In 2009, the Carnegie Corporation of New York's Council on Advancing Adolescent Literacy, under the direction of Harvard's Catherine Snow, issued its capstone report on the current state of affairs. The first paragraph of the first page is as follows:

Overall, we are failing to create highly literate, college and career ready adults with the literacy skill sets that qualify them for employment in the new global knowledge economy. The most recent data shows poor performance by U.S. students compared to many other nations (UNESCO Institute for Statistics, 2003, 2007). Although U.S. students in grade four score among the best in the world, those in grade eight score much lower. *By grade ten, U.S. students score among the lowest in the world.* (Carnegie, original emphasis)

A New Direction

Why are so many students finishing high school with weak writing skills? Kelly Gallagher makes the following observation: "Certainly there are a number of factors out of our immediate control (e.g., poverty, lack of parental involvement, second language issues). Dwelling on these issues, however, is counterproductive and a waste of time and energy. . . . we are better served by focusing on what we can control—namely, our teaching" (6–9).

Let's face it: teaching writing is hard work. The problems are often vexing, students are often not very interested in or responsive to our efforts, and progress is often glacial. Many years of teaching composition have shown me that the following three areas, generally omitted from or minimally covered in the writing curriculum, can go a long way toward making writing classes interesting, making instructional efforts transfer to improved writing skills, and making newly acquired skills carry over from year to year.

1. Show students how humans read, that is, how they process written material. Without this information, students are not as well prepared to produce text that is conducive to that process. Additionally, many of the rules and requirements that we cover in the composition classroom make better sense to student writers if they have a minimal understanding of how our brains process written material.

2. Show students how to read like writers, that is, how to analyze texts to see what makes them work (or fail), and then help students incorporate some of the more useful structures and techniques into their own writing. Early in her excellent text *Strategic Writing*, Deborah Dean notes that "student writers need to learn strategies for understanding how texts work and strategies that help them replicate aspects of texts in different contexts. Students need strategies for reading texts, contexts, audiences, and purposes" (9). If

exposure to these strategies incorporates how the brain processes written language, the strategies make better sense and are therefore more teachable.

3. Take advantage of the knowledge about spoken and written English that our students—native speakers, advanced non-native speakers, and Standard English learners (SELs)—bring with them into the classroom. As Ken Lindblom notes, "Students don't come to us broken. They don't need to be fixed. They come to us with vast experience as language practitioners—and they have accomplished a great deal by using language effectively" (*English Journal* 100.4 11). This vast storehouse of information is a rich, yet terribly underutilized resource that's just sitting there, waiting for us English teachers to tap into and take advantage of.

The Brain Game

Borrowing a line from the *Declaration of Independence*, I hold these truths to be self-evident:

- Education is at the center of what teachers are all about.
- Reading and learning are at the center of education.
- The brain is at the center of reading and learning.

If you find no fault with those statements, then the following statement should be equally acceptable.

> Understanding how the brain reads and learns will put writing teachers in a better position to help our student writers prepare material that feeds the reading (and learning) process.

In the writing classroom, we are dealing with three different sets of brains:

1. **Readers' brains.** Katherine Perera notes that a twelve-year-old reads at an average speed of 200 words per minute, or three to four words per second (128). The proficient adult is, of course, even faster. Writers must create material that feeds this rapid-fire process. What do writing students need to know about how the reading brain processes language? What signals, structures, and devices facilitate this swift processing? What might slow down or confuse the reader?

2. **Students' brains.** Babies are born knowing next to nothing about the new world they have just entered. Yet, a few years later, they come to our classrooms in control of a truly phenomenal body of knowledge about objects, actions, society, language, and so on. They have acquired most of this body of knowledge from nothing more than exposure, without the benefit of structure or professional guidance. How can we writing teachers take advantage of this tremendous storehouse of knowledge that our students possess? How can we build from what they already know about language to what they need to know about writing?

3. **Teachers' brains.** What do English teachers need to know about the functioning of the first two sets of brains in order to more efficiently and effectively prepare and present material to help student writers better master the writing process?

This text addresses all three of these sets of brains, showing how to take advantage of some of the "hidden" resources that they contain.

Book Overview

Many of the concepts that we try to teach our students in the composition classroom are hard to explain or demonstrate. However, once students have a basic idea about how the reader's brain processes written material, these concepts become much more accessible, much more logical, and therefore much more teachable.

I begin, therefore, by examining how a proficient reader processes written material, but from a nontechnical perspective. The first two chapters contain truly interesting, easy-to-grasp demonstrations that provide insights into how humans process written material. These chapters also offer plenty of classroom activities and exercises that help students apply the insights gained from their new understanding in order to improve their organizational skills. Chapter 3 puts these newly discovered concepts to further use, as it demonstrates and explains the roles of the various components of an essay from a reader's perspective. Chapter 4 reverses the process: it shows student readers how to analyze writing in order to see what good writers have done to feed the reading process, with an eye toward helping students incorporate some of these same findings into their writing. Chapters 5 and 6 narrow the focus to the sentence and paragraph, respectively. Chapter 7 expands back out to the essay level, looking at more holistic aspects such as voice and genre. Finally, Chapter 8 explores the application of these concepts to dialectically diverse students, more commonly referred to as nonstandard English speakers or SELs.

Chapter Structure

All too often these days, teachers, harried and hassled by the demands of their profession, want quick fixes. "Just show me exactly what to do in my classroom, and I will go back and do it. Maybe. If I agree with it. And if I can find the time." Teaching is part art, part science. Perhaps someday things will be so thoroughly automated that teaching becomes purely formulaic: plug in the right Lego pieces and the structure will be permanently erected. However, at least for the foreseeable future, such a scenario belongs in the realm of science fiction.

If teachers understand *why* certain activities and approaches are effective, they will be better able to remember them, to use them effectively, and to improve on them. In the words of Eric Jensen, one of the pioneers in the field of brain-based learning, "[I]f you don't know why you do what you do, it's less purposeful and less professional" (6). To help build toward that end, each chapter of this book is broken down in this way:

- The general thrust and direction of the chapter sets the stage for the activities, demonstrations, and discoveries that follow.

- The theoretical underpinnings for a specific area or activity provide background for *what* is being covered and, often, *why* it is advantageous.

- Classroom activities or demonstrations show how to present the concept(s) to your students.

- Each chapter closes with a discussion of the information that you want your students to understand as a result of the classroom activity or demonstration.

- Classroom applications offer additional exercises, games, and so on that you can do with your students to expand or reinforce the targeted teaching point(s).

Settle back, get comfortable, and get ready to explore the exciting possibilities that present themselves once we examine how readers read and, to a certain extent, how student writers learn. This book contains a wealth of challenging—and interesting—material that will help you advance your students' writing skills to the next level.

Feeding Reading

Imagine that someone has to prepare fuel for an engine, but that person has no idea about the internal processes that take place when the fuel is burned. She might be able to produce a fuel that would allow the engine to sputter along, but she might also produce a concoction that could shut the engine down. One thing is certain: she would not be in a very good position to maximize the engine's potential unless she knew something about what the engine does with the fuel. This situation is analogous to that of student writers. They are tasked with providing fuel (pieces of writing) that can be processed efficiently by engines (readers' brains). If writers have a basic idea about how the brain processes writing, they will be better able to provide material that could make these engines "run" more efficiently.

Please don't misunderstand me: I do not mean to say that our students must be reading experts before they can learn to write effectively. What I mean is that student writers need to have some fundamental, easily grasped knowledge about how readers process writing. Once they have this basic understanding, they are much better able to understand *why* certain techniques work, *why* certain rules exist, and *how* certain parts of the whole function. They are also in a better position to see why some of the things that they do when they write might confuse or confound the reader.

Student writers can readily understand the basic concepts concerning how a proficient reader reads if they are presented with simple, yet truly fun and interesting demonstrations. These concepts should be established as early as possible in the semester or school year. They will then serve as a backdrop to your ongoing instructional efforts. Let me walk you through the demonstrations, and then we'll discuss how they can help students become better writers.

Some information in this chapter was previously published in Crow ("Feeding Reading").

The Proficient Reader

If you asked people on the street how proficient readers read, most people would probably agree that readers' eyes run smoothly across each line of print from left to right (in this culture), drawing each of the words into their brains to be processed for meaning. This basic understanding is wrong on two counts: eye movement and word-for-word reading.

Eye Movement

The first general misunderstanding of the reading process has to do with how our eyes move as we read.

Classroom Demonstration: Eye Movement

- Pair up your students and have them sit facing each other. (Try this yourself—a partner is not required. Just follow the instructions and tune in to your own eye movement rather than watching someone else's.)
- Tell person A: Look straight ahead—do not move your head in any direction.
- Tell person B: Observe your partner's eye movement carefully as you follow these instructions. (If you don't have a partner, perform each of the following steps on yourself.)

  1. Take a pencil and hold it up on one side of your partner's face. Ask your partner to move his eyes only, so that he can see the pen or pencil.

  2. Move the pencil *slowly* from one side of your partner's face to the other, asking him to follow the pencil with his eyes as it moves.

  3. Now put down the pencil and ask your partner to move his eyes to one side, and then to move his eyes *slowly* to the other side, as if he were following the pen or pencil. *Slowly* is the key word. If the person moves his eyes quickly from one side to the other, nothing is noticeable.

- Tell persons A and B: Reverse your roles.

(If you are doing this experiment yourself, don't read any further until you complete the steps just outlined, feeling how your eyes move at each step.)

This simple experiment demonstrates a basic, yet surprising fact about our eyes: the human eye cannot move smoothly in any direction—left, right, up, or down—unless it is locked onto and following a moving object. If there is no moving object, the human eye moves in a series of small, jerky jumps (called *saccades*, although I don't use this term with my students). A line of print is not a moving object, so proficient readers *cannot* scan smoothly across each line; their eyes move across the page in a series of jumps. Want to drive yourself crazy? Think about it as you continue to read this text!

So why is this important to student writers? You'll see—it is one piece of an important concept concerning the reading process.

Word for Word?

The second general misunderstanding of the reading process has to do with how proficient readers process words. When proficient readers read something, do they truly process all of the words that it contains? Let's find out.

Classroom Demonstration: Word for Word 1

Prepare a transparency, a PowerPoint slide,[1] or a piece of paper with the sign shown in Figure 1.1. (I recommend that you perform this experiment on yourself by reading the sign according to the following instructions, but don't look at the sign until you have read the instructions.)

- Ask your students to remain quiet during this demonstration. A few may have already seen what you are about to do; even if nobody has seen it, you don't want comments from others to spoil the effect.

- Tell the students that you are going to flash up a sign—just long enough for them to read it. Ask them to read it silently and then answer a couple of questions.

- Show the sign for about two seconds. (If you are performing this experiment on yourself, turn to the next page, glance at the sign *once*—just long enough to read it—and then continue reading.)

FIGURE 1.1. Sign to read.

- Ask students if they had enough time to read the sign. If some did not, show them the sign again, briefly.
- Ask students to hold up their hands if they agree that the sign says PARIS IN THE SPRING.
- Ask the students who don't believe that the sign says PARIS IN THE SPRING to hold up their hands.
- Inform the class that the sign does *not* say PARIS IN THE SPRING.
- Repeat the process, flashing the sign to your students until everyone sees what it actually says.

This demonstration provides good evidence that we do *not* read text word for word. If we processed each word serially as we read, it would be impossible to miss the second "THE." Normally, however, more than half of your class will not see it the first time. In fact, I often have students who are embarrassed because they continue to miss it. Other students have to tell them, or I have to say, "Read the sign carefully, *word for word*." Then I show the sign for as long as it takes them to read it. When they finally see the second "THE," I congratulate them on being very proficient readers! (Appendix A has a full-page version of this sign for you to use with your classes.)

Classroom Demonstration: Word for Word 2

Here is another exercise, easily found on the Internet, that will demonstrate to your proficient readers that they are not processing the written language word for word. Try it yourself. The instructions are simple: read the following sentence once at your normal speed, counting all of the *F*s that you see in it as you read.

> FINISHED FILES ARE THE RESULT OF YEARS OF SCIENTIFIC STUDY COMBINED WITH THE EXPERIENCE OF YEARS.

Most readers find three *F*s in the sentence. In reality, there are six. Good readers usually miss the *F*s in the three occurrences of the word *OF*. Why? Sentences contain a combination of *content words*—words filled with meaning—and *function words*—words required because of the structure of the sentence and the vocabulary it contains. In English, it so happens that we use the word *of* in all three of these phrases: "are the result of," "years of," and "experience of." There is no logical reason for using *of* here—it's just what we do in English. We could, for example, easily say "are the result from" or "by"; we just don't. Your brain, trained by countless hours of exposure to English, knows these pairings very well, so it pays scant attention to *of* in contexts like this. This boils down to *economy of effort (EofE)*—your brain takes all of the shortcuts it can while processing incoming data. We'll deal with the concept of economy of effort often in this book, beginning with the next section.

Sample-Predict-Confirm

Here's what you want your students to understand from these demonstrations: proficient readers do not scan smoothly across a line of print, processing every word they encounter. Instead, their eyes jump across the line, they *sample* what's there, and they *predict* what comes next. As long as subsequent reading *confirms* their predictions, they continue to read. If predictions are not confirmed, processing halts, and the reader goes back to reread the passage more carefully, trying to figure out what went wrong. The following classroom demonstrations will develop this analysis of the reading process and allow your students to see why it applies to writing.

Classroom Demonstration: Erroneous Prediction

So that your students (or you) can experience what it feels like to make wrong predictions while reading, take a look at the following sentence. If you are going to write the sentence on the board for your students to read, ask them to look away until you finish writing. In order to experience the effect, they need to process the sentence in its entirety rather than word by word as you write it.

The dog returned to its owner was happy.

The reading processor that you have tucked away in your brain, which I refer to metaphorically as your *reading brain*, was thrown off because it predicted that "the dog" was the subject of "returned," making "The dog returned to its owner" combine into a well-formed sentence. But when your reading brain hit "was," you failed to confirm your predicted structure and were forced to reread the sentence—perhaps several times. Had I not removed two words ("that was"), your reading brain would have made perfect predictions:

The dog that was returned to its owner was happy.

economy of effort

A proficient reader's reading brain is a finely tuned machine that breezes through reading passages, expending as little energy as possible (EofE) as it interacts with written text and extracts meaning from it. Right now, computer scientists can only dream of creating a text processor that can match our capacity for understanding the written word.

Incidentally, one's reading brain does not do sample-predict-confirm processing in single units. It might be confirming predictions made in a previous cycle while it predicts from the newly processed passage as it samples from the next passage, and so on. So proficient reading calls for the simultaneous processing of several sample-predict-confirm sequences.

Reading is one of the most challenging tasks that we require of our conscious brains. And yet the machinations are, for the most part, unexamined by the vast majority of readers. Stanislas Dehaene notes that "reading has become so automatic as to be inconspicuous: as an expert reader, you concentrate on the message and no longer realize the miracles that are worked out by your brain" ("Your Brain").

Unless you have a classroom filled with problem readers, your students' reading brains are a valuable resource for you, the writing teacher. The sample-predict-confirm process is an important case in point. Once your students grasp this process, a new, critically important area makes itself available to you. Let's see why this whole business is so crucial to and useful in the composition classroom.

The GUESS Error

We want our readers to process the fruits of our writing labors smoothly and effortlessly. Because readers sample-predict-confirm as they process text, writers need to be able to produce text that ensures that predictions are confirmed. Therefore, if a writer creates material that gives rise to erroneous predictions, the writer is usually to blame. This type of writing error is indeed a serious one. I call it a *GUESS error*, capitalizing GUESS because, as you will see, this is a special kind of "guess."

Classroom Demonstration: Professional GUESSing

If a passage is well written, readers should be able to make good GUESSes; that is, they should be able to predict the general (and often specific) content and direction of the text. Following is the beginning of a passage taken from a fourth-grade sample reading assessment ("Huge Bones"). I have divided the passage into segments so that you can pause to make predictions and then see how well you did. Here is the process that I strongly encourage you to follow. I will discuss how to present the same material to your classes later.

- Take a sheet of paper and cover the passage. Then slide the paper down until you see [GUESS].
- Read up to that point, and make your prediction about what the writer will discuss next. (More than one prediction is perfectly acceptable; for example, it might be this, or it might be that.)
- Slide the cover sheet down until the next [GUESS] is exposed.
- Continue this process until you complete the short excerpt.

Huge Bones Make Big Hit!

What's bigger than a school bus and has teeth up to 12 inches long? **[GUESS]**
It is Dinosaur Sue! **[GUESS]**
Sue is a Tyrannosaurus rex, or T. rex. **[GUESS]**
She is on display at the Field Museum of Natural History in Chicago. **[GUESS the next paragraph]**
     This colossal dinosaur skeleton is named after Sue Hendrickson, **[GUESS]** the scientist who discovered it. **[GUESS]**
The enormous skeleton is 41 feet long. **[GUESS]**
[The paragraph continues with more facts about the dinosaur.]

Because this passage is properly tied together, you were probably able to make very good GUESSes. You couldn't GUESS the exact content each time; indeed, at some points, more than one perfectly reasonable GUESS was available. The first sentence in the second paragraph serves as a good example of this last point:

> This colossal dinosaur skeleton is named after Sue Hendrickson, the scientist who discovered it.

Two logical GUESSes can be made here:

1. You might GUESS that more information about Sue Hendrickson follows.
2. You might GUESS that more information about Dinosaur Sue follows.

Either GUESS is perfectly logical. But if the author's next sentence dealt with, let's say, the eating habits of a T. rex or, even more bizarrely, the price of tea in China, the author would have made a GUESS error. That is, the author would have made a shift that was not supported by the flow and logic of the text—one that *nobody* would have expected, and one that would throw a monkey wrench into any reader's sample-predict-confirm processing.

Sometimes, the general sense of the passage helped you with your predictions. Yet on at least one occasion, punctuation was the primary source: the comma after "Sue Hendrickson" sent a signal to your reading brain that allowed you to GUESS that more information about this lady was coming next.

(I chose a fourth-grade passage just to illustrate that this whole GUESS concept is readily accessible to elementary student readers. Obviously, the same concept applies to any coherent reading passage, irrespective of level or complexity: the writer is obliged to organize things so that the reader can make good GUESSes.)

Classroom Demonstration: Student GUESSing

Here is a passage taken word for word from the introduction to a student essay. The passage is copied and pasted exactly as I received it. The only change I made was to break it into GUESS segments. Cover the passage with a piece of paper, and slide it down until you see the first [GUESS].

Introduction to Student Essay

In life, things don't get easier, and things are not handed to you. **[GUESS]**
I would love to do anything having to do with sports. **[GUESS]**

My competitive softball team played at the national tournament and won first place. **[GUESS]**

Softball relaxes me. **[End of introduction—GUESS what this essay is about]**

This essay is from a college (yes, college!) freshman student. Ask your students the following questions:

1. What kind of impression do you have of this writer? On a scale of 1 to 10, how would you rank her in terms of intelligence, organization, attention to detail, and college readiness?
2. Would you want this person on your *Jeopardy* team?
3. If you were an employer, would you hire this person?

This student turned out to be a very articulate, intelligent young woman. Yet the impression that she creates with this piece of writing leads one to believe just the opposite. Unfortunately, she committed a cardinal sin: she wrote this at 3:00 a.m. on the day it was due and handed it in at 8:00 a.m., without even reading it over once. When I showed her what she had done, she was horrified!

In this example, the first two GUESS errors would have been resolved for the reader if the third sentence had somehow connected the general concept of "sports" with "things not being easy" or "things not being handed to you." When the third sentence starts yet another thread in the discussion, the reader is lost. The most damaging problem of all, though, is that after reading the entire introduction, the reader *does not know the specific focus or direction of the essay*. In other words, the reader is not prepared to interact with the text and make nicely targeted sample-predict-confirm sequences when processing this student's essay. Ouch! A fundamental function of an introduction is to prepare the reader to make intelligent GUESSes while reading. This student author tosses the reader straight into the body of the essay without proper preparation. We'll return to this important point in Chapter 3 when we discuss introductions and conclusions.

The GUESS concept provides a tangible way to help students grasp the critically important but rather esoteric terms *coherence* and *cohesion*. Students have a terrible time trying to identify with or understand these terms and the concepts they embody. And no wonder: normally, when we teach cohesion or coherence, we tend to violate one of the basic axioms of writing: *show, don't tell*. We *tell* our classes about cohesion and coherence problems, *tell* them where these occur in their writing, and *tell* them that readers cannot understand the text. The GUESS error concept allows you to *show* students where cohesion or coherence breaks down, *show* them what happens to the reader, and, as a result, *show* them why what they wrote doesn't work. So the GUESS error concept is a tangible way to present cohesion and coherence—one that students can identify with and readily understand.

Classroom Application: GUESS Errors

GUESS error presentation methods. Here are four ways to present GUESS errors to your class:

1. Cover sheet: Give each student (or group of students) a copy of the GUESS exercise, but hand it out upside down, with the blank side of the page on top. Instruct the class to put a cover sheet over the printed side of the handout, turn over both the handout and the cover sheet, and slide down the cover sheet (just as you did when you were introduced to the earlier GUESS exercises) until they see the first [GUESS].

2. Overhead projector: Make a transparency of the GUESS exercise, cover it with a piece of paper, and slide the paper down to reveal each GUESS segment.

3. PowerPoint slide: Make each segment of text (up to a [GUESS]) into a bulleted item or a separate text box on a PowerPoint slide. Then use the Custom Animation feature to make all but the first one appear on separate mouse clicks. You can lead the discussion with your students about possibilities for each of the segments, revealing the next one with the click of a mouse.

4. Word document: Prepare the exercise as a Word document, skipping a line between each GUESS segment. Leave the first segment of every GUESS example unchanged. Highlight the remaining segment(s) of each GUESS example, and change the font color to white. The print will disappear. Project this image, lead the discussion, and then triple-click with the mouse in the area where the next text is probably located. A triple-click will highlight the entire next segment. Once the segment is highlighted, change the font color to black, and it will "magically" appear.

The GUESS concept in peer evaluations. Spotting GUESS issues lends itself nicely to peer work. Have students use a word processing program to convert part or all of their rough drafts into GUESS exercises. Ask each student to print out the result and bring it to class. Pair off the students, and have them take turns doing the other person's GUESS exercise orally, using the cover sheet method described earlier. If a partner makes a bad GUESS or is unable to GUESS, ask her to explain why. This activity often leads to rich and insightful discussions between the participants—almost irrespective of their individual writing levels. Problem areas can be referred to you, the teacher, or presented to the class for discussion and resolution.

GUESS errors in submitted writing. When you see GUESS errors as you go through student papers, mark them for the students, and keep a collection of them (anonymously, of course). If you have an electronic copy of an essay with errors, copy and paste enough context into a separate document to allow students to see the breakdown. If you are working with papers, then type the excerpt into the document. Here are three examples from some of my students' past writing efforts.

Example 1

[First sentence in the introduction] Eating, sleeping, and laughing should be a part of our daily lives to stay healthy, but **[GUESS]**
…but what is it that we eat every day?

This is a great example of a student writer who is trying to narrow the focus, trying to bring the reader to his topic, but who omits a step in the process. There is nothing in this first sentence that allows the reader to GUESS that "eating" is the main focus. Instead, readers GUESS that the contrast that "but" presages will apply to all three of the named items—something like ". . . but we do not get enough of them." GUESS errors like these are common in introductions. When the entire class fails to GUESS how the sentence ends, the student writer is presented with tangible evidence of the problem. Letting the class work together to resolve the writing issue allows the author to see how to solve the problem and can help her as she crafts future introductions.

Example 2

[Introduction] Financial aid is an important factor when trying to select a college to attend. It is important for many reasons. One reason is to help families that cannot afford to send their children to school. **[GUESS]**
Scholarships, loans, and work-study are just a few common types of financial aid given to students to help them through college. [End of paragraph]

This author spends *two sentences* setting up readers to GUESS a list of reasons—and then he provides only one! As written, there are two viable directions to take at this GUESS juncture: (1) either provide more information on family financial constraints (and then give a second reason) or (2) give a second reason. Further, because the writer says there are "many reasons," there must be at least three reasons in this introduction. Because this is not the direction the writer wants to take, he could change "One reason" to "The primary reason." But the reader still isn't in a good position to GUESS what comes next, so a transition sentence would be helpful.

Example 3

[New paragraph] Imagine that you are a particularly resilient fisherman, able to withstand the cold water and the terror of being pulled overboard. You must look up towards the surface as you are dragged deeper and deeper towards your impending death. Do you grab at the rope around your ankle in a futile attempt to save yourself? Do you scream your last breath or do you hold it until you pass out? **[GUESS]**

Temptingly enough, it is not unheard of for crab fishermen to make 10,000 dollars a month.

This last sentence comes at the reader out of nowhere. Nothing in the preceding text prepares the reader for this major shift in topics, a fact that will be clearly demonstrated when the entire class is blindsided by this GUESS exercise. This sentence undoubtedly made sense to the writer within the context he had set up in his own mind, but readers are not privy to that context. Writers must step outside of their own minds and view things from a reader's perspective. The GUESS concept provides a vivid way to demonstrate this idea for your students.

Major surgery for GUESS errors. Here is a good way to return to the GUESS concept several days after you have introduced it. Divide your class into small groups, telling each group that it is a team of surgeons. Ask each group to appoint a lead doctor. The group is to examine a "patient"—a short passage that contains a GUESS error. Inform the group that the patient has been diagnosed with a bad case of GUESS error disease. Their first task is to determine the location of the disease. The group must then perform major surgery on the patient, restoring it to good health (that is, repair the GUESS error, making it easy for the reader to process). You can give every group the same patient or, if your collection is extensive enough, give each group a different one. Then have the groups present their findings and discuss their surgeries. (I refer to all of my students as Dr. [Last Name or First Name] during this entire exercise.)

Classroom Activity: Round-Robin Writing

This is a time-honored classic that fits nicely into the GUESS lesson plan. Tell the class that they are going to create a story. Inform them that, before writing a new sentence, each student can read *only the previous sentence*. Hand one student a piece of paper with numbered lines. The first line contains sentence 1, which you have created to get things started. The first student writes sentence 2 to the story, and then folds the paper so that only 2 is visible. The third student reads sentence 2 only, writes sentence 3, and folds the paper again so that only 3 is visible. Continue this process until eight to ten students have contributed. (Have the rest of the class involved in some other activity that can be interrupted.) Then read or display the story to the class, showing the problems that inevitably arise.

Note: If you have an overhead projector, turn off the projector and have students write their story on a transparency, covering the previous sentences as you go. If you have a computer hooked to an LCD projector, turn off the projector and have the students write on the connected computer, hiding the previous sentences as you go along. To hide a sentence, highlight it and change the font color to white. When you are ready to display the work to the class, highlight the entire document (Ctrl + A) and change the font color back to black.

As a variation, the next time you do this activity, allow students to read the previous two sentences before adding to the story. Then do it again, allowing them to read the three previous sentences. Here is the normal result from this activity:

- Seeing only the previous sentence will cause rampant GUESS errors.
- Seeing the previous two sentences will produce kinder, gentler GUESS errors.
- Seeing the previous three sentences will result in a fairly cohesive passage.

When you go over these activities in class, ignore or downplay misspellings, grammar errors, and so on. The idea is to concentrate on how the text builds (or fails to build) from beginning to end. So the discussion should center on what happens to readers as they attempt to process the passage. Sometimes, this exercise will result in a passage that is too disjointed to be repaired. Sometimes, fairly simple changes—the addition of a single word or phrase, or the restructuring of sentences—will resolve problem areas. Work together with your students to figure out how the passage can be improved so that readers can sample-predict-confirm easily as they process the text.

Reading like Writers

When you write, you draw on a wellspring of knowledge, much of which you acquired through lots of exposure to well-written material. Most of your students, however, have not had nearly as much exposure. Every new crop of students seems to have read less professionally written material than the previous year's crop. Students today are multiliterate; that is, they read blogs, text messages, emails, wikis, social networking sites, and so on. Their exposure to well-crafted writing comes primarily from school assignments, not only in English language arts classrooms, but in all content areas. That exposure, of course, increases as they rise through the grades.

Unless students have serious reading deficiencies, they are able to read and understand professionally written material. In other words, they are in *receptive control* of well-written material: they can decode it when they see (or hear) it. Their *productive control*, that is, their ability to *produce* well-written material, lags considerably behind their receptive abilities. When they read, they are subconsciously processing the well-written material with little, if any, awareness of the techniques and structures that were used to create it.

If our students read more for pleasure, more of the craft of good writing would be absorbed through an osmosis-like process, thereby becoming a part of their productive skill set, just as it undoubtedly did for you. However, most of today's students are not getting this extended exposure, so we teachers must help them *discover the craft that good writers use*. We must help them become consciously aware of techniques that good writers employ, and help them incorporate these techniques into their writing. In other words, we must help students learn how to read like writers so that they become more skilled at writing for readers.

An excellent way for students to begin to incorporate the craft of creating cohesive writing is to examine passages in order to discover what the authors have done to help readers make good predictions. The following activity forces students to zero in on how authors tie pieces of a paragraph together to make it cohesive. We will examine other ways to reveal strategies and craft in professional writing in subsequent chapters.

Classroom Activity: Reconstructing Transitions

I'll introduce this activity to you in the same way I introduce it to my classes—by modeling it. Following is an exercise that was created from a paragraph that I chose almost at random from *Time* magazine (Gorman et al.). (I say "at random" because virtually any well-written passage that you choose will be suitable for this type of exercise. I chose *Time* for this demonstration because I know that my audience here consists of educated individuals who are proficient readers.) Your job is to match the sentence beginnings (numbered) with their endings (lettered). Put the proper letters in the blanks after each sentence beginning. We'll talk about how you were able to perform this task after you complete the exercise.

Paragraph 1

1. [A person's name] has dyslexia, _____.

2. It's _____.

3. Yet _____.

4. Indeed, _____ _____.

   a. it is so hard for skilled readers to imagine what it's like not to be able to effortlessly absorb the printed word
   b. the exact nature of the problem has eluded doctors, teachers, parents and dyslexics themselves since it was first described more than a century ago
   c. a reading disorder that persists despite good schooling and normal or even above-average intelligence
   d. a handicap that affects up to 1 in 5 schoolchildren
   e. that they often suspect the real problem is laziness or obstinacy or a proud parent's inability to recognize that his or her child isn't that smart after all

Here is the original passage:

[1] [A person's name] has dyslexia, a reading disorder that persists despite good schooling and normal or even above-average intelligence. [2] It's a handicap that affects up to 1 in 5 schoolchildren. [3] Yet the exact nature of the problem has eluded doctors, teachers, parents and dyslexics themselves since it was first described more than a century ago. [4] Indeed, it is so hard for skilled readers to imagine what it's like not to be able to effortlessly absorb the printed word that they often suspect the real problem is laziness or obstinacy or a proud parent's inability to recognize that his or her child isn't that smart after all.

Let's examine our sample exercise sentence by sentence.

1. [A person's name] has dyslexia, *a reading disorder that persists despite good schooling and normal or even above-average intelligence*. The main part of the sentence ends at "dyslexia," and you could, in fact, use a period instead of a comma and have a well-formed sentence. The comma lets your reading brain know that something is being added to the end of this sentence. Your

reading brain intuitively expects, or GUESSes, that the addition contains more information about dyslexia, so it's the perfect place for a definition of the term.

2. It's *a handicap that affects up to 1 in 5 schoolchildren.* Your reading brain knows that "It" refers to "dyslexia," allowing this sentence to be connected to the previous one. Your knowledge of English sentence structure helps you select the proper ending. Note that the endings for sentences 1 and 2 are almost interchangeable. It makes a bit more sense, though, to put the definition of "dyslexia" (c) first, followed by the statistic (d).

3. Yet *the exact nature of the problem has eluded doctors, teachers, parents and dyslexics themselves since it was first described more than a century ago.* "Yet" signals the reader that some information is coming that runs counter to what one might expect, thereby connecting this sentence.

4. Indeed, *it is so hard for skilled readers to imagine what it's like not to be able to effortlessly absorb the printed word* . . . "Indeed" indicates that what comes next is information that emphasizes or strongly supports the information in the preceding sentence. Then, when you reach "the printed word," your knowledge of English sentence structure lets you know that this sentence is not complete.

5. Indeed, it is so hard for skilled readers to imagine what it's like not to be able to effortlessly absorb the printed word *that they often suspect the real problem is laziness or obstinacy or a proud parent's inability to recognize that his or her child isn't that smart after all.* The beginning of this sentence establishes a pattern with which your reading brain is very familiar: "It is so X that Y." Once you spotted that familiar pattern, you were able to GUESS both the general content that was coming and its structure. (Of course, the process of elimination made it easy for you to join this last phrase to its stem, but it would have been very easy to select this ending if it had appeared somewhere in the middle of the choices.)

Model this activity before turning your students loose to do it on their own. Use a *gradual release of control* approach, which Stuart Greene summarizes: "we can teach strategies directly by *modeling* the process of analyzing discourse features, giving students opportunities to *practice* individually or in groups, and then gradually *fading,* so that students are actively engaged in their own learning" (42).

1. Teacher Only: Do a passage or two for the students, thinking out loud to help them see how you approach the task.

2. Teacher + Class: Do a passage with the students, asking them as a class to help you put the paragraph back together. As answers are suggested, ask the students to explain how they made their choices. You may have to give some hints or gentle guidance along the way, of course.

3. Class Only: Let them do it on their own in small groups.

After a bit of practice to accustom students to this type of thinking, they will get the hang of it.

The discussions generated by this exercise are rich and productive. We humans normally ignore or take for granted the things that bind a text together; making students consciously aware of the craft of joining thoughts together rather than merely processing text for meaning has two advantages:

1. Students will begin to "see" new ways to tie information together when they write.

2. Students will gain a better feeling overall about how good writing is structured, and about how good writing truly feeds reading.

Classroom Application: Extending the Reconstruction

Do it yourself. Have students prepare their own exercises by choosing interesting paragraphs from a Web article. They can copy and paste these into a word processing program and move things around as required to create the reconstruction exercises. Be sure to tell students to leave the first sentence intact to establish context. Then pair up the students, and have them exchange papers and work on each other's exercise.

In-depth analysis. The paragraph that was used in the exercise from the *Time* article provides several areas—patterns or structures—that you could zoom in on. Once you have played around with one or more of these, ask students, during revision, to find a place in their drafts to use such patterns or structures. Here are three examples from this paragraph:

1. Appositives: Sentence 1 ends with an appositive that is used to provide a definition of a term. This is a great opportunity to present the use of appositives, having students mimic it, and so on. Let students contrast the professional version with a more amateurish two-sentence version.

   • Original: [A person's name] has dyslexia, a reading disorder that persists despite good schooling and normal or even above-average intelligence.

- Two-Sentence Version: [A person's name] has dyslexia. Dyslexia is a reading disorder that persists despite good schooling and normal or even above-average intelligence.

2. It is so X that Y: Let students play a bit with the pattern found in sentence 4 (imitating it, combining sentences, and so on). Then require that they find a place to use this pattern in their writing.

3. Series Repetition: In sentence 4 the author has a series in which he repeats the conjunction: ". . . the real problem is laziness or obstinacy or a proud parent's inability . . ." Ask students why the author repeated "or" in this series, and how the feeling would change if he had chosen to write this as a simple series: ". . . the real problem is laziness, obstinacy, or a proud parent's inability . . ."

We will examine the reading-like-writers concept in greater detail in subsequent chapters.

Summary

The following concepts were introduced and demonstrated in this chapter.

- **Feeding reading.** Because writers are preparing material for readers to process, having a basic understanding about how readers process material will help students create writing that is conducive to that processing. Eye movement and word-for-word reading demonstrations were used to shed light on how a proficient reader processes text using sample-predict-confirm cycles.

- **The GUESS error.** If a piece of writing is properly structured, the reader should be able to make good GUESSes about what comes next. Establishing reader expectations and then violating them creates a GUESS error, a common problem in student writing. Classroom applications of this basic concept were examined.

- **Reading like writers.** Professionally written material is a treasure trove of strategies, techniques, and structures that readers process without paying conscious attention to them. Bringing a writer's craft to the conscious attention of student writers helps them to incorporate some of the concepts into their own writing. This chapter explored transitions and their value in helping to avoid GUESS errors.

Further Reading

For a classic analysis of the reader as a non-passive participant, see Kenneth
Goodman's "Reading: A Psycholinguistic Guessing Game."

For a present-day peek inside the reading brain, see Stanislas Dehaene's *Reading
in the Brain*, where you will find (among other things) an analysis of how,
according to brain research, children learn to read.

Note

1. If you use PowerPoint, put a blank slide before and after the one containing the sign,
   so that you can move quickly in either direction away from the sign.

2

Economy of Effort and the Self-Googling Brain

Your brain has truly phenomenal processing resources at its disposal as it takes care of its daily affairs. However, these resources are not infinite; although the storage capacity of the brain is vast,[1] there are severe limits to the amount of information that it can deal with at any point in time. Therefore, your brain has developed some very clever ways to minimize the amount of data that it must manipulate as it processes incoming information. *Economy of effort (EofE)* is a driving force in the brain's handling of external data and accessing of internally stored data, a phenomenon that cognitive scientists frequently refer to as *cognitive economy*. Kathleen Berger defines the concept very simply: "Cognitive economy means the most efficient and effective use of mental resources" (478). EofE is not something that the individual can turn on or turn off; the brain automatically applies EofE "shortcuts" all over the place.

Because reading is a very intense, resource-hungry process, EofE comes into play constantly as proficient readers process text. Proficient writers need to produce material that facilitates EofE processing. In Chapter 1 we explored one of the brain's fundamental EofE shortcuts in reading: the sample-predict-confirm cycles that allow proficient readers to skip over words and phrases as long as the predictions that earlier samples generate are confirmed by subsequent reading. In this chapter, we will examine some other EofE shortcuts and see how they can be used in the writing classroom.

The Self-Googling Brain

The human brain is a phenomenally interactive organ. Not only does it interact with external events and all of your body's other organs, but it also interacts with itself: it is "hyperlinked" to information that it has stored in various locations in both brain hemispheres. For example, merely seeing (or hearing) the word *cat* causes your brain to google itself for information related to that word.

You can instantly recall

- what cats look like.
- what a cat feels like (if you've ever handled one).
- what cats like to eat.
- what noises cats make.
- what it smells like if you fail to change the kitty litter.
- what experiences—pleasant or unpleasant—you have had with cats.
- what you named your pet cat(s) (if you had any).

This list is certainly not all-inclusive, but it suffices to make my point: when your brain sees or hears a word, it is able to tap into a whole network of information that came from a variety of senses and experiences. It brings this information from the various storage locations to the forefront, making information more easily accessible if you need it in order to understand or react to what you are reading (or hearing). This ability is a phenomenal feat, one that even the most powerful computers in the world can't begin to replicate. This facility is what I call the *self-googling brain*: the brain's ability to automatically search itself for and access related information.

Understanding EofE and the self-googling nature of the brain helps student writers better comprehend how to anticipate the needs of their audience and, to a certain extent, how to organize and structure their writing in order to facilitate reader interactions with it. Plus, students find the subject matter truly interesting—an unbeatable combination.

Classroom Demonstration: Humans versus Computers Part IA

This is the first of a two-step process that demonstrates the self-googling nature of the human brain. I have done this activity with second graders through college students, and they all got it immediately—and had fun with it! (The sentence that I use for Parts IA and IB comes from an article by Pat Carrell [106].)

Here are the basic directions for Parts IA and IB:

- Divide your class in half. Tell one half that they are humans, and tell the other half that they are computers.
- Show the class the following sentence:

    The policeman held up his hand and stopped the car.

- Ask the following questions:

1. Humans, was there a driver in the car? (They will, perhaps hesitatingly at first, agree that there had to be one.)

2. Computers, was there a driver in the car?

   a. If your computers say yes, ask them to show you where the sentence states that fact.

   b. If your computers say no, ask them to show you where the sentence states that fact. (As you can see, the only answer a computer could give is "Insufficient information" or "Don't know.")

- For the remaining questions, ask the humans first and then the computers:

3. Were the brakes used to stop the car?

4. Did the policeman touch the car with his hand when he held it up?

5. In what position did the policeman hold his hand when he held it up?

6. What was the policeman wearing?

The humans will answer every question easily; the computers will give the same boring non-answers. Why can we humans accomplish this task so readily? As soon as our brains hear "policeman," they google themselves for information and experiences associated with the concept of *policeman*, bring that data to the forefront, and interpret the sentence in light of this body of knowledge.

Classroom Demonstration: Humans versus Computers Part IB

Now make a simple change to the target sentence. Replace the subject of the sentence as follows, and then repeat the six questions from Part IA, substituting "Superman" for "policeman."

Superman
~~The policeman~~ held up his hand and stopped the car.

The humans will change all of their answers; the computers will provide the same boring non-answers. Why? Because as soon as the readers' brains processed the word *Superman*, they self-googled for information pertaining to this new entity, brought this new information "to the top," and reinterpreted the sentence accordingly. Present-day computers cannot begin to imitate the incredible flexibility of the brain in tasks such as these, but human readers (and listeners) do it effortlessly.

Schemas and Scripts

Your brain contains amazingly complex, detailed bodies of knowledge called *schemas*[2] that it has put together based on your experiences. A schema is defined as "an internal representation of the world; an organization of concepts and actions that can be revised by new information about the world" ("Schema"). So, in the earlier demonstrations, when your humans self-googled, they accessed their policeman schema and could immediately supply a lot of detail that was not provided by the text. When the subject changed from policeman to Superman, they accessed a different schema—one, in fact, that students a hundred years ago would not have had—and the entire scenario suddenly changed.

Classroom Demonstration: Humans versus Computers Part II

Parts IA and IB, showed the self-googling brain in action at the sentence level. Now let's look at the paragraph level.

For this demonstration, switch positions: tell the humans that they are now computers, and vice versa. Then read the following paragraph, asking them all to listen carefully.

> While visiting New York City, Jim took his wife Jane to a fancy French restaurant. With a lot of assistance from the waiter, he ordered a complete three-course meal for the two of them. However, when the server brought him the bill, Jim was shocked by how much the total was. He left vowing never to go to another French restaurant.

- Now ask each group of students the following questions:
  1. Humans, does Jim speak French? How do you know?
  2. Computers, does Jim speak French? (Again, the only acceptable answer is that the computers don't know—they have insufficient information.)
- For the remaining questions, ask the humans first and then the computers:
  3. Did Jim and Jane actually eat the meal?
  4. How did they eat the food—with chopsticks? With their hands?
  5. Did the table have a tablecloth and cloth napkins?
  6. What was the server wearing?
  7. Did Jim actually pay the bill?

8. (Ask the humans this question first, but before you ask the computers, stage whisper the answer: 60.) How many words were in the paragraph that I just read?

9. (Stage whisper the answer only to the computers: 329.) How many letters and spaces were in the paragraph that I just read?

In Part II we see a *script* in action. A script is a course of action—what normally transpires in a given situation. In this demonstration, your students know what takes place in a restaurant: you are seated, order your meal, eat it, pay for it, tip the server, and so on.

When you read (or listen), the brain brings entire bodies of experience—different scripts and schemas—to the fore, so that the reader (or listener) can interact with the text. In this demonstration, the brain tapped into at least one script and two schemas: how things transpire in a restaurant (a restaurant script), how a restaurant looks (a restaurant schema), and how a certain type of restaurant looks (a French schema). The brain also made *inferences* as the story unfolded. For instance, you knew that Jim probably didn't speak French very well because he needed so much help from the waiter to order the meal.

Of course, you may have students in your class who have never been to a fancy restaurant, French or otherwise. These students may have inadequate scripts and schemas for fancy restaurants, so they may not be able to answer some of the questions. However, by the time students reach middle school, they have probably seen people in movies or on television eating in fancy restaurants, so even though they may not have had a fancy restaurant experience themselves, they will have fairly well-developed fancy restaurant scripts and schemas.

Demonstrations like the ones presented here help writers appreciate the importance of taking audience into careful account. One of the reasons that writing is so difficult is that writers must decide *in advance* how much information their readers bring to the table. If writers underestimate their audience and stuff too much information into the text, readers will be bored or irritated; if they overestimate their audience and don't provide enough details, readers will be lost.

Rather than *tell* students over and over that they have to take their audiences into account, these demonstrations *show* them one very important reason why they must—the reader's self-googling brain.

Inferences

Another way to help students understand the importance of audience is to have them read a short passage and then compile a list of inferences that their brains easily made, as well as the scripts and schemas that their brains brought up.

Classroom Activity: Inferences

David Rumelhart and Andrew Ortony provided a three-line "story" that serves as an excellent resource for examining inferences, scripts, and schemas.

- Divide your students into small groups (two to four students).
- Tell students that the author of a story that you are about to show them has taken audience into account and intentionally left out lots of details.
- Show the groups the following three-line story, instructing them to fill in the gaps—to make a list of the inferences they made and the scripts and schemas they accessed as they read it.

  [1] Mary heard the ice cream van coming.

  [2] She remembered the pocket money.

  [3] She rushed into the house. (qtd. in Eysenck 392)

Here is a list of some of the inferences that readers make (unconsciously) when they read these three short sentences. None of this information is explicitly provided in the text—computers would not be able to come to any of these conclusions:

- Mary wanted some ice cream.
- Mary needed some money.
- Mary did not have any money with her.
- Her pocket money was in the house.
- Her pocket money was enough to buy the ice cream.
- Mary had a limited amount of time to complete the transaction.
- Mary lives in the house into which she rushed.

At least three schemas and scripts were brought into play: an ice cream schema, an ice cream van schema, and a purchasing script. These scripts and schemas allow the reader to know information such as the following: the van had a freezer of some sort; Mary heard the van coming because it was broadcasting a song as it moved; and, if Mary got her money in time, she handed at least some of it to the driver who, in turn, gave her some ice cream and some money back if necessary. This background knowledge and the inferences it enables allow the reader to fill in the gaps in the story. So the author presented a very small piece of the overall picture—the bones, as it were—and the readers' background knowledge, accessed by their self-googling brains, provided the meat.

And so it is with everything we read: the author provides a fairly minimal amount of information (not quite as minimal as in the contrived ice cream example, of course!), and the readers' brains provide much of the detail, leaving the readers with a richer understanding than the mere words, alone, convey.

What if the author were writing this story for people who live deep in a jungle along the Amazon River? He or she would have to supply a lot more detail about ice cream, ice cream vans, and purchasing, given that these might not have been part of the audience's experience. Being aware of the background information that the audience possesses is a critical component to take into account when writing. Inferences, scripts, and schemas are an excellent way of demonstrating this important concept.

Classroom Activity: Changing Audiences

Divide your class into small groups. Ask each group to brainstorm a list of details they would have to include in order to make the previous three-sentence story, repeated here in paragraph form for your convenience, intelligible to a community of people who live deep in the jungle along the Amazon River. Here is the paragraph:

> Mary heard the ice cream van coming. She remembered the pocket money. She rushed into the house.

Once they have compiled their lists, ask your class, either as a group or as individuals, to write the new version of the story. You could also play around with genre here. Because this hypothetical group of people probably has little idea about what life is like in your students' society, the story might seem foreign to them. So you could, for example, ask the students to write the story as a fairy tale.

Alternatively, because the possibilities for these kinds of stories are boundless, you could ask students to come up with their own three- or four-sentence paragraphs that would require knowledge of life in U.S. society—knowledge that our hypothetical Amazon River residents would not possess. Then have students rewrite their own versions as described earlier.

Rewriting stories for a group of people very different from your own is an excellent way to establish and reinforce the concept of audience and its importance in the writing process.

Additionally, this type of activity can be useful when you don your reading-teacher hat: it demonstrates clearly how readers are not passive recipients of information when they read; instead, they draw heavily on the background information stored in their brains. In other words, readers don't simply extract meaning from texts; they *interact* with texts and come away with a deeper understanding of a passage than the words themselves relate.

Self-Googling: A Problem for Writers

An issue that plagues novice writers is their inability to step outside of their own heads and view the passage from their readers' perspective. We implore our students to do so, to take their audience into careful account, and to remember that readers are not privy to the same information that writers have floating around in their heads. The problem once again is that we are *telling* our students. The self-googling facility and the script, schema, and inference concepts provide us with opportunities to *show* them what we mean—in genuinely interesting and compelling ways. Here's how I summarize things for my students:

> As we write, our own brains are constantly self-googling, accessing information (facts, episodes, scripts, and schemas) that has been placed there by our experience, and bringing that information to the top so that it is readily available. Normally, this facility is wonderful. It allows us to weave complex tapestries of thoughts and concepts from minimal texts (written or spoken). If our brains were not capable of such marvelous feats, writers (and speakers) would have to put forth incredibly detailed accounts or information, slowing communication down to a crawl. However, as writers, and especially as novice writers, this facility often *interferes* with the ability to communicate rather than helping it.

Remember the student writer whose introduction we examined as a GUESS exercise in Chapter 1? She was the softball player whose team had won first place in a national tournament. Her introduction made perfect sense to her when she wrote it, but was verging on utter nonsense to you when you read it. Why was there such a huge disconnect? The answer is obvious: within the context of her self-googling mind, the introduction was crystal clear; however, you didn't have access to her thoughts when you read it. She had failed to take her audience into account, failed to step outside of her head and view things from a reader's perspective, and had produced a GUESS error disaster as a result.

Classroom Activity: Thinking about Audience

Table 2.1 shows various types of writing and names two different audiences for each. Describe how you would change the vocabulary and the content of your writing in order to help each audience access and understand the information that you are trying to relate. The first one is done for you.

Chunking

Earlier in this chapter, we saw three EofE "tricks" that the brain uses: self-googling, the ability to make inferences, and the schema/script organizational structure. Let's examine another EofE concept that plays a vital role in writing: *chunking*.

When information enters our conscious brains, it is held temporarily in *short-term memory (STM)* until it can be further processed and either forgotten or stored, depending on its perceived importance. STM has two important, self-limiting characteristics.

1. STM is temporary: information disappears quickly. Left unrehearsed, information in STM fades away within about fifteen seconds.

2. STM is finite: it can hold approximately seven pieces of data (Eysenck 293); anything beyond that causes overload.

Classroom Demonstration: Chunking

In his insightful book *Why Don't Students Like School?*, Daniel Willingham presents a quick but effective way to demonstrate the concept of chunking. Try it yourself before presenting it to your class.

- Tell your students to get paper and pencil ready. You are going to briefly show them a grouping of letters. They are to read through this once, and then write down the letters exactly as they saw them. They cannot begin writing until you say "Go!"

- Either project the following or print it out in a font large enough for the entire class to read. Show it for just a few seconds, take it away, and say "Go!"

TABLE 2.1. Thinking about Audience

Type of Writing	Audience 1	Audience 2
Product Advertisement **Goal:** Sell the product	**Teenagers** **Vocabulary:** Use slangier, funnier language and more graphics. **Content:** Highlight features that appeal to young people.	**Senior citizens** **Vocabulary:** Use more sophisticated language and a more serious tone. **Content:** Highlight features that benefit older people.
Campaign Speech **Goal:** Get elected	**Military** **Vocabulary:** **Content:**	**Farmers** **Vocabulary:** **Content:**
Movie Review **Goal:** Make people want to go see the movie	**Adults** **Vocabulary:** **Content:**	**Families** **Vocabulary:** **Content:**
Magazine Article **Goal:** Inform readers about an event	*Time* magazine **Vocabulary:** **Content:**	*People* or *Us* magazine **Vocabulary:** **Content:**
Encyclopedia Entry **Goal:** Inform readers about a person	**Adults** **Vocabulary:** **Content:**	**Children** **Vocabulary:** **Content:**
Job Application **Goal:** Get hired	**Graphic Artist** **Vocabulary:** **Content:**	**Office Manager** **Vocabulary:** **Content:**
Biography **Goal:** Write a book about a famous person that will sell well	**General** **Vocabulary:** **Content:**	**History Scholars** **Vocabulary:** **Content:**
Travel Poster **Goal:** Make people want to go to a location	**Middle Income** **Vocabulary:** **Content:**	**Upper Income** **Vocabulary:** **Content:**

Learning to Write for Readers: Using Brain-Based Strategies by John T. Crow © 2011 NCTE.

XCN

NPH

DFB

ICI

ANC

AAX

Your students (and you, if you tried this yourself) will find this task virtually impossible.

- Now inform your students that you are going to repeat the experiment, but this time with a different grouping of letters. The same set of instructions apply. Here is the new set:

X

CNN

PHD

FBI

CIA

NCAA

X

Your students will be much more successful with this group than with the previous one.

The eighteen letters in both sets are identical. In the first grouping, the spacing does not allow you to tie any of the eighteen letters together in a meaningful way, so you are forced to remember each one individually. Eighteen distinct items are well in excess of the STM capacity of seven, so your memory quickly overloads, and you fail at the task. The second spacing puts the letters into recognizable groupings—acronyms—so that they can be readily chunked; in other words, multiple letters can be conflated into a single item to remember. For example, NCAA reduces the load on STM because four entities (the letters) chunk into a single entity (the acronym or "word"). As a result, the list of eighteen individual items becomes a list of seven chunked items, so the load is much more manageable. As Willingham notes, "[T]he amount of space in working memory doesn't depend on the number of letters; it depends on the number of meaningful objects" (26).

Notice, however, that each chunking cannot occur unless you have prior knowledge of the acronyms. If, for example, you are not from the United States, or if you are not a fan of college sports, then NCAA might be meaningless to you. In that case, the four letters would not conflate, so chunking could not occur. In fact, before presenting this list to your students, you should make a judgment call about whether all of your students would know all of these acronyms. If you think that one or more of the items may be unfamiliar, then substitute your own (OMG, IMHO, or LOL are pretty safe bets with today's texting crowds).

Your brain is able to chunk all kinds of information—EofE at its finest! For example, champion chess players are able to chunk entire boards, but novices must remember the relative positions of all of the pieces. Mathematicians can chunk large pieces of a mathematical formula, allowing them to recall amazingly complex formulas with relative ease.

Because most sentences are longer than seven words, readers (or listeners) have to be able to chunk words into phrases, and phrases into clauses, while reading or listening; otherwise, their short-term memories would quickly overload. In fact, the previous sentence contains 35 words—well in excess of your STM capacity of 7, yet you processed it with ease, without overburdening your STM, because you could chunk it. Again, it isn't the number of *words* in a sentence that determines working memory load—it's the number of meaningful *units* (phrases and clauses). Writers must provide readers with signals along the way to help them know *where and how to chunk*. (Punctuation is the primary signaling device that writers have at their disposal to perform this task, but a detailed examination of punctuation as a guide to chunking is beyond the scope of this book.)

Background Knowledge

Background knowledge is any information you have stored in your brain that pertains to a subject area. Included in this broad term are retained facts, images, sounds, tastes, smells, episodes, scripts, schemas, and skills that you have accumulated as you have gone through life. Your brain makes this truly massive body of information available to you as you read, enabling you (as we saw earlier) to comprehend much more than the mere words of a passage convey.

Classroom Demonstration: Background Knowledge and Memory

The influence of background knowledge on one's perception and recall was vividly demonstrated in a classic 1932 study by L. Carmichael, H. P. Hogan, and A. A. Walker (cited in Baddeley, Eysenck, and Anderson 96). Your students will enjoy replicating it in the classroom (see Figure 2.1).

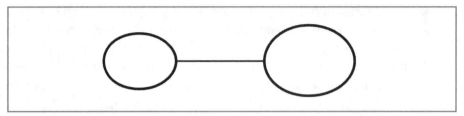

FIGURE 2.1. Basic graphic image.

- Prepare two copies of the graphic in Figure 2.1, making each big enough to show or project to your class. In each image, be sure to make one circle noticeably larger than the other, and put some distance between them. Label one image "Eyeglasses" and the other "Dumbbells." Otherwise, they should be identical.
- Divide your class in half, and ask one half to close their eyes. Show the other half the image labeled "Eyeglasses" for two to three seconds. Don't say anything about expectations—just show them the image.
- Reverse the process with the other half of the class, showing them the "Dumbbells" image.
- Wait a day or so, and then ask your students to draw the images they saw. Many of the student drawings will be influenced by the label that was associated with the image. (See Figure 2.2 for possible results.)

Students in this setting have an advantage over the subjects in the Carmichael study. The original subjects viewed several images, one right after the other, and then were asked to redraw all of them immediately; your students see only one. However, the time lapse erases at least part of their advantage.

Although both sets of students were shown the identical graphic image, their recall will be influenced by the associated label. Most students will draw circles

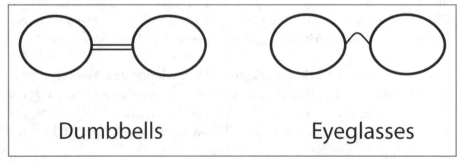

FIGURE 2.2. Typical student versions.

of the same size, and they will probably put them closer together than in the original image—especially in the "Eyeglasses" group. In addition, the line joining the two circles may be affected depending on the label the students viewed. These are "mistakes" that a computer would never make. Humans make them because of EofE: rather than attend to the careful details of the image, the brain draws on its experience with each of the named objects and normalizes the image to the named shape. It's easier (EofE) to match the input to an already existing image than it is to retain the details of a new one, so that's exactly what most people do.

This demonstration should help your students understand what readers do when they process text. It's vitally important that writers express themselves clearly, concisely, and concretely, with plenty of details to help readers form the proper memories as they interact with the text.

Classroom Demonstration: Optical Illusion

So far, we have looked at how EofE and language interact as the brain processes information. But EofE comes into play no matter what the data source is, an important concept to keep in mind in this age of visual literacy. The following optical illusion (Talusan and Chen) provides a good illustration of EofE with visual input.

Show your students Figure 2.3, telling them that this is the background image for the next two images. Two of the lightly shaded diamonds, numbered 1 and 2, are the points of interest in this demonstration.

FIGURE 2.3. Background image.

Figure 2.4 shows a computer analysis of the color components of both diamonds. To a computer, all colors, including shades of gray, are numbers.

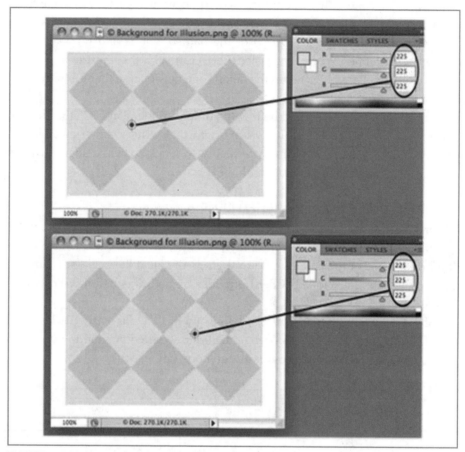

FIGURE 2.4. Background image analyzed.

Colors are created by combinations of red, green, and blue (RGB). Photoshop, a popular photo-editing tool, allows you to break down any point in a graphic image into its RGB components. Figure 2.4 shows the Photoshop analysis when the cursor is placed in each of the two targeted diamonds. They are identical in color: 225 red, 225 blue, and 225 green.

Now show your students Figure 2.5, and ask them which diamond looks hazy and which looks sharp. Then show Figure 2.6 and ask students the same question. They will reverse their answers, even though the diamonds in all three figures are *the identical shade of gray*. Why? EofE.

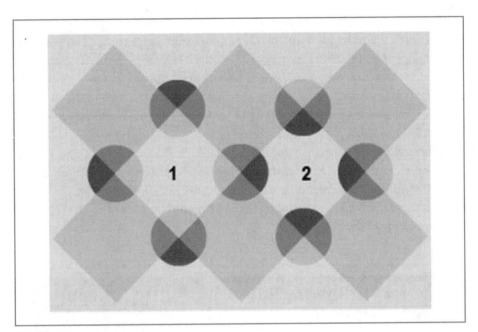

FIGURE 2.5. Hazy version A.

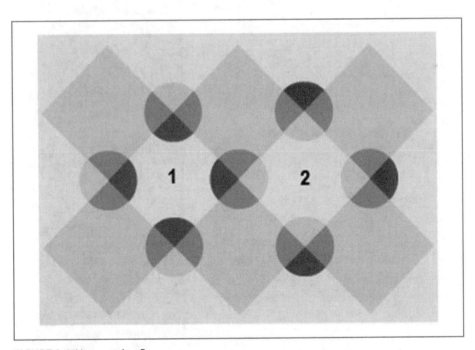

FIGURE 2.6. Hazy version B.

The same background image was used in both "hazy" versions, so diamonds 1 and 2 are the identical shade of gray. Any haziness that you perceive is a product of your brain, not the reality of the graphic images. The computer, of course, is not fooled by the shading. Photoshop shows that the actual shade of gray for diamonds 1 and 2 does not change in any of the images. In all of the graphics, the shade of gray is created by 225 red, 225 green, and 225 blue (see Figures 2.7 and 2.8).

When shaded circles are superimposed on the background image so that diamond 1 is surrounded by lightly colored segments of the circle (Figure 2.7), the diamond itself appears to be hazy in contrast to its neighbor, which is surrounded by darkly colored segments. When the situation is reversed, the "haziness" moves with the circles.

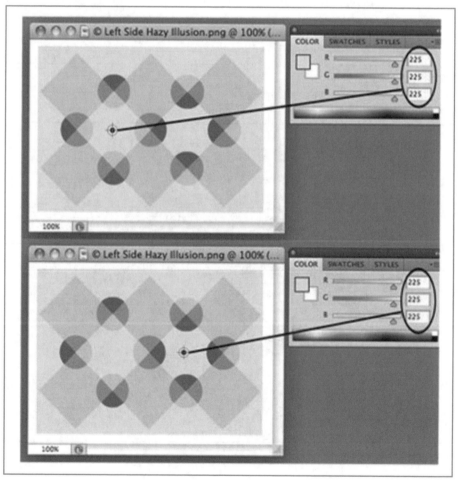

FIGURE 2.7. Hazy version A analyzed.

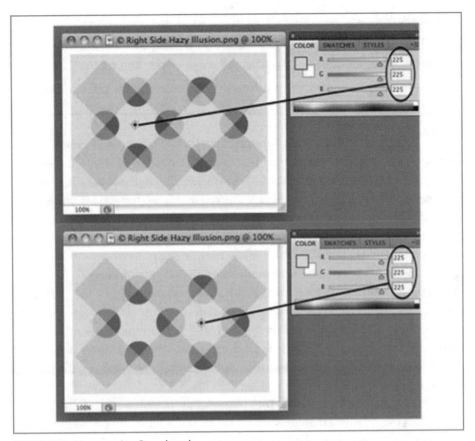

FIGURE 2.8. Hazy version B analyzed.

EofE is most certainly at work here. Your brain does not analyze every square millimeter of everything that you look at. Your brain understands how lighting, layering, patterns, and shadows work, so in Figure 2.7, the shading leads your brain to believe that diamond 1 must be superimposed on the circles, an interpretation supported by the shading of the remaining figures (a sort of visual sample-predict-confirm). That superimposed diamond can't be transparent—it must be blocking part of the light. So that's exactly how you perceive it—hazy-looking. The shading also convinces your brain that there is no diamond 2. Reverse the shaded circles (Figure 2.8), and the hazy appearance reverses also.[3]

Economy of Effort and Writing

As we discussed earlier, the same EofE that is such an indispensable aid to rapid-fire reading and listening makes the writer's job all the more difficult.

- Readers do not carefully process every word that one writes.
- The understanding of a text is heavily influenced by the reader's background knowledge (scripts, schemas, experiences, and so on).
- The understanding of a text is heavily influenced by the inferences that a reader makes during processing.

So, if one were to do a fine-grained analysis of different readers' understanding of and reaction to a given text, no two would be absolutely identical. Therefore, writers are shooting at a moving target: they want to provide enough information and details to allow the reader to conjure up the proper images and make the desired inferences, but they must not overexplain lest they bore or irritate readers.

Understanding the EofE nature of the brain aids students when they write, by helping them appreciate the absolute necessity of the following.

Stepping outside of their own heads. Writers can't control the EofE processing that their brains perform as they write. Writers' brains are constantly self-googling, and the results of their "searches" will undoubtedly differ—perhaps subtly and perhaps grossly—from the results of their readers' self-googling efforts. Writers can't expect readers to understand their text based on the context inside their own brains.

Letting their work grow cold for at least a day. If writers reread the product of their labors soon after they finish writing, all of the self-googled, newly stimulated information remains fresh in their minds. They need to let it percolate, and let other self-googling searches supplant it across at least a twenty-four-hour period. Only then can writers hope to read their own writing with relatively fresh eyes.

Having outside readers. If students truly understand the self-googling nature of their brains, then this one is self-explanatory.

Taking the reading process into account. If readers can't chunk properly, or if they can't make good GUESSes, then writers have seriously flawed products. Further, knowing how readers process writing, and understanding the signals that they need for this processing, will help student writers understand the logic of many of the conventions of writing that are otherwise so difficult to explain. (We'll examine this area in more detail in Chapter 3.)

Taking audience into careful account. Historically, getting students to seriously consider audience has been a tough sell. However, knowing that readers don't simply extract meaning from a text, but that they *interact* with it, employ EofE processing, and derive their own interpretations provides an obvious, solid rationale for thinking carefully about audience.

Revising. Many student writers resist revision. Their years of exposure to oral communication is certainly part of the problem: people don't worry about getting it right the first time in a conversation because feedback from their listeners allows them to clear up misunderstandings and problems on the fly. Speaking is a social act; writing, in one sense, is a solitary act. So writers must examine their products from a variety of angles, trying to ensure that they have communicated clearly and concisely, taking into account the variety of perspectives that their audience might bring. To further complicate matters, writers must make a good impression on their readers with proper voice, diction, grammar, and so on. As Mark Twain famously advised, "The time to begin writing an article is when you have finished it to your satisfaction."

Summary

The following concepts were introduced and demonstrated in this chapter.

- **The self-googling brain.** As we read, our brains automatically find stored information that is relevant to the words or concepts that we are reading about, and then bring this information to the top. We explored how this facility of the brain is critical in order for readers to grasp the full intent of a passage and why it is often problematic for writers.

- **Schemas and scripts.** A schema is information about a concept organized into an interlinked grouping for easy access. A script is information about how to behave or interact in a given situation. So, for example, we have a classroom schema that allows us to recall details about a typical classroom, and we have a classroom script that informs us about the behavior and activities that typically take place in a classroom.

- **Inferences.** Readers draw all kinds of inferences—make judgments or draw conclusions—as they read. Schemas and scripts combine to allow humans to make these inferences and, as a result, to understand *much* more about a passage than is actually expressed by the words or sentences it contains.

- **Economy of effort (EofE).** The brain's capacity for analyzing data at any point in time is limited. In order to conserve these precious resources and speed up processing, the brain has developed shortcuts that allow it to minimize the amount of data it must process, a facility we refer to as economy of effort.

- **Chunking.** One of the brain's EofE tricks is its ability to conflate two or more separate items into a single unit—or chunk—to relieve the load placed on short-term memory. We saw how the brain chunks language data as well as visual data.

Further Reading

For an analysis of what's wrong with today's schools from a cognitive scientist's perspective, see *Why Don't Students Like School?* by Daniel Willingham.

For a detailed examination of chunking as it pertains to writing, see my book *Unleashing Your Language Wizards*.

For a careful review of long-term memory, short-term memory, and learning, see *Memory* by Alan Baddeley, Michael Eysenck, and Michael Anderson.

For a review of schemas, scripts, and their effects on reading, see *The Psychology of Language* by Trevor Harley.

For a thorough analysis of background knowledge as it pertains to reading, see Douglas Fisher and Nancy Frye's *Background Knowledge*.

Notes

1. Paul Reber makes the following estimate: "neurons combine so that each one helps with many memories at a time, exponentially increasing the brain's memory storage capacity to something closer to around 2.5 petabytes (or million gigabytes). For comparison, if your brain worked like a digital video recorder in a television, 2.5 petabytes would be enough to hold three million hours of TV shows."

2. The Greek form of the plural, *schemata*, is also used instead of *schemas*.

3. To see these changes take place in a video, go to http://web.mit.edu/persci/gaz/main-frameset.html and click on "Haze Illusion."

Reader Expectations and the Essay

Chapters 1 and 2 provided ways for students to see that readers do not enter into the reading process as passive participants. Instead, they bring their experience and background knowledge into the equation and interact dynamically with the text. A critical job for the writer, therefore, is to structure text that facilitates the reading process, that is, to tie a piece of writing together to enable readers to make good GUESSes—a process referred to in Chapter 1 as feeding reading. Many of the concepts that are taught as part and parcel of good writing (title, introduction, thesis statement, topic sentence, and so on) are included because of the significant role they play in helping readers process the written word. The feeding reading perspective that was developed in the previous chapters will allow you, the English language arts teacher, to demonstrate to student writers how the various pieces of an essay aid readers as they process text. Or, equally as compelling, this perspective will allow you to demonstrate what can happen if these pieces are missing or mishandled. This chapter examines each of these features from the feeding reading perspective, providing demonstrations and activities to help your student writers understand their contributions to the efficient and effective processing of text.

The Power of the Title

Getting students to assign a title to each essay can sometimes be a struggle; getting them to create one that truly helps the reader prepare for the written passage can be a battle royal. The following demonstration, taken from research into human cognition, will help your students understand the importance of a title. Follow the instructions as you try this yourself, and you will see a vivid manifestation of the power of a title on your interaction with a passage—and so will your students when you take this demonstration into the classroom.

Classroom Demonstration: Title Insurance

Tell your students that they are about to hear a paragraph titled "The Prisoner." Write this title on the board. Then read the paragraph to the students.

> Rocky slowly got up from the mat, planning his escape. He hesitated a moment and thought. Things were not going well. What bothered him the most was being held, especially since the charge against him had been weak. He considered his present situation. The lock that held him was strong, but he thought he could break it. He knew, however, that his timing would have to be perfect. Rocky was aware that it was because of his early roughness that he had been penalized so severely—much too severely from his point of view. The situation was becoming frustrating, the pressure had been grinding on him for too long. He was being ridden unmercifully. Rocky was getting angry now. He felt he was ready to make his move. He knew that his success or failure would depend on what he did in the next few seconds. (Bransford and Johnson 719)

Ask your students if they had any trouble understanding the general contents of the paragraph. They will probably agree that it was easy to follow.

Now tell them that you are going to read a paragraph with a different title. Cross out "The Prisoner" and write "The Wrestler" on the board. Then read the same paragraph again.

When your brain was exposed to the word *prisoner*, it self-googled and brought to the top any background information that it had stored about prisoners. Your brain then interpreted the paragraph in light of that information. As a result, ambiguous words such as *mat, lock, escape,* and so on were assigned meanings that were in keeping with the background information (scripts and schemas) that you had acquired about convicts, causing you to make inferences that were consistent with this information. When your brain was exposed to the word *wrestler*, it brought up an entirely different set of background information (scripts and schemas) that caused you to assign new meanings to the ambiguous language, thereby radically altering your interpretation of the paragraph.

This demonstration will be a real eye-opener for your students. They will be able to *feel* how a title can alter the reader's GUESSes, inferences, and interpretation. This paragraph is, of course, an extreme example, carefully contrived by the researchers to allow them to examine how humans process language. Yet this demonstration very clearly shows the potential that a good title has to prime the reader's brain and influence her preparedness for and understanding of the content.

The Role of the Introduction

The primary role of an introduction can be summed up in one word: GUESS. Obviously, there should be no GUESS errors within the introduction itself. More important, however, after readers have finished processing the introduction, they should be able to GUESS what the essay is about—perhaps in general terms or perhaps very specifically—with absolute accuracy.

Students are more likely to make GUESS errors in the introduction than in any other part of an essay. Let's look briefly at the two types of GUESS errors that student writers make.

1. **Disjointed GUESS.** As student writers attempt to write an introduction that adequately prepares their readers, they often fail to interconnect their thoughts properly. All of the details are well connected in their heads, of course, but they lose sight of the fact that their readers do not share their mental contexts. So, in their attempts to zero in on their thesis statements, students tend to jump from thought to thought, without bringing the reader along. Their thoughts may be logically ordered, but are placed in the paragraph like beads on a necklace, leaving the reader unpleasantly surprised by what comes next and wondering how things interrelate. The Bad Introduction 1, which follows, provides an excellent example of this phenomenon.

2. **Underprepared GUESS.** Although we teach the concept of introduction and thesis statement, we don't *show* students what happens when readers are not properly set up for the body of the essay. The GUESS concept allows us to demonstrate very clearly the difference between underprepared and well-prepared readers prior to reading the body of an essay. Here is a critical point to drive home: *If the reader cannot GUESS the general content and direction of an essay after reading the introduction, the writing is seriously flawed.* The following demonstrations and follow-up activities will help reinforce this point.

Classroom Demonstration: The Bad Introduction

I have a rather large collection of introductions with GUESS errors, gathered from years of classroom teaching. We examined some of them in previous chapters. Here are two others. Have your students follow the GUESS exercise process as described in Chapter 2.

The Bad Introduction 1

The group of animals that I will focus on is reptiles. **[GUESS 1]**

When I say cold-blooded animals, many think that these types of animals are always cold, but what really happens is that their body depends on the temperature of the environment. For example, when it's warm and the sun is out, reptiles get hot and usually more active. **[GUESS 2]**

Like humans, reptiles have lungs that allow them to breath, but unlike humans most of them lay eggs. **[GUESS 3]**

These can include snakes, turtles, alligators, and many others. **[GUESS the general direction or content of this essay 4]**

First of all, none of this information belongs in the introduction. The first sentence informs us that the author is writing about reptiles. He then provides specifics about reptiles that he later repeats in his essay, an unveiling that is somewhat analogous to showing someone a gift she is going to receive just before gift wrapping it. The purpose of an introduction is to prepare the reader, to provide background information, perhaps, but *not* to supply specific details that will be in the body. However, let's ignore the fact that most of this information is misplaced, and look at the GUESS errors that this introduction contains.

The GUESS error concept demonstrated in this introduction provides a tangible way for you to show students that they have committed any of the following three crimes, which are all felonies, not misdemeanors.

1. They have failed to step outside their heads and view their writing from the reader's perspective.

2. They have failed to provide necessary transitions.

3. They have failed to properly prepare the reader for the content of their essays.

GUESS 1. This is a great example of failure to process the passage from the reader's perspective. The writer's brain has googled up a context that he sees very clearly; he is writing as if his readers were in there with him, sharing his thoughts. They aren't. "When I say" is a poor transition because, obviously, he has yet to introduce the concept of cold-blooded anywhere except in his own mind.

GUESS 2. Nothing exists in the text to inform the reader that the writer is in the process of listing facts about reptiles or comparing them to humans. Without a transition, the normal GUESS would be "When it is cold outside, ..." The writer needs some sort of transition device to bring readers along, rather than blindsiding them with an unexpected shift.

GUESS 3. At the very least, the writer needs a transition here. Even so, this general sentence should be placed much earlier in the paragraph—probably after the first sentence. The GUESS perspective clearly shows that it would fit there.

GUESS 4. As noted earlier, this is the most serious error of all. Once they have finished reading this introduction, readers cannot GUESS where this essay is heading. They know that the author is writing about reptiles, but they have no idea about the general content, direction, or purpose of this writing.

The Bad Introduction 2

When a person decides to have genetic testing done, the results must remain confidential between the doctor and the patient. Issues may arise in one's life depending on the results of the genetic testing. The importance of making an informed decision when choosing to have testing done is invaluable. **[GUESS the general direction or content of this essay]**

This introduction raises more questions than it answers. Is the author writing about the importance of confidentiality? The importance of an informed decision? Issues that may arise? How to make an informed decision? How to choose the testing? The stage has certainly not been adequately set to prepare readers to interact with the content of the essay—wherever it may be headed.

Classroom Demonstration: The Good Introduction

To demonstrate the impact of a well-written introduction, show students the following example.

The Good Introduction

Imagine the following scenario: You come home from work and enter the living room. In the room, you find your son, who is seven years old, sitting with an older man. The man is dressed in a suit, clean-cut, and doesn't look like he is going to harm your son. Yet still, he is a stranger who has convinced your son to let him into your home. The man has been entertaining your son and they have quickly become friends. Your son is intrigued to learn more about this man. He watches him as if hypnotized, and views him as a role model. Your son quickly decides that he wants to be like this man. Everything seems to be very innocent. I leave you to imagine how you would react, but I'm sure you wouldn't invite this man to stay for dinner. Just as the man took control of your child's innocence, so do TV commercials.

If you were to ask your students what this essay is going to be about, everyone would have the same general answer: how television commercials mislead children. They would also be able to make intelligent GUESSes about the content and general direction of the next paragraph.

Although it's true that the author's use of an analogy is an effective way to introduce her position in this piece of persuasive writing, that is not the point here. The point is that, because of her introduction, readers have self-googled good information; their brains are properly primed; and they are ready to interact with this text, make good GUESSES, and process it smoothly (assuming the body is as well written as the introduction). Contrast how well prepared readers are this time with the floundering that they experienced with the previous two introductions. A well-constructed introduction is a powerful weapon, indeed, for getting readers properly situated to interact with the contents of one's writing.

Why do students have such a hard time writing good introductions? One common cause is the way the writing process is traditionally taught. The introduction should be the *last* thing a writer creates, not the first thing. I will return to this important point in Chapter 7, "Exploring the Concept of Essay."

Classroom Activity: GUESS from the Introduction

- During revision, pair off your students.
- Have Student A read his introduction to Student B. (Reading the introduction allows Student B to tap into her abilities with spoken English. Therefore, the reading level or writing ability of Student B is inconsequential.)
- Ask Student B to GUESS the general subject and direction of the body of the essay. If she makes a bad GUESS or is unable to GUESS at all, then Student A might have some work to do.
- Next, have Student A GUESS from Student B's introduction.

Also encourage your students to ask outsiders—family members or other friends—to GUESS after their introductions.

The Role of a Topic Sentence or Thesis Statement

From a feeding reading perspective, the difference between a topic sentence and a thesis statement is minimal.

A *topic sentence* prepares the reader for the content of a paragraph.

A *thesis statement* prepares the reader for the content of an essay.

Because they are so similar, I'm going to lump them together here.

Professional authors often don't use either device when they write. Further, if they do use these devices, they may not put them in the standard places (at the beginning of a paragraph or at the end of an introduction, respectively). Think about your own personal writing process: when you change to a new paragraph, do you think, "Okay, first I have to write a topic sentence"? Of course not! And yet that's exactly what we often ask our students to do. Are we wrong, then, to require a topic sentence or thesis statement? I don't think so.

Experienced writers have an inner sense of organization, topic maintenance, coherence, and cohesion. Student writers often lack that inner judgment. I inform my students that they do not have to use topic sentences or thesis statements as long as their writing works; however, I strongly encourage them to do so until they get more experience under their belts.

Classroom Demonstration: Do What?

(If you want to do this experiment yourself, do not look at the asterisk note until you read the targeted paragraph.)

- Divide your class in half. Call one half the "experimental group" and the other the "control group."
- Show the experimental group the sentence that is in the asterisk note.* The control group sees nothing.
- Then read the following paragraph to everybody.

    The procedure is actually quite simple. First you arrange things into different groups. Of course, one pile may be sufficient depending on how much there is to do. If you have to go somewhere else due to lack of facilities, that is the next step; otherwise, you are pretty well set. It is important not to overdo things. That is, it is better to do few things at once than too many. In the short run this may not seem important, but complications can easily arise. A mistake can be expensive as well. At first the whole procedure will seem complicated. Soon, however, it will become just another facet of life. It is difficult to foresee any end to the necessity for this task in the immediate future, but then one can never tell. After the procedure is completed, one arranges the materials into different groups again. Then they can be put into their appropriate places. Eventually they will be used once more, and the whole cycle will then have to be repeated.

However, that is part of life.(Bransford 134–35)

* Doing the laundry is not difficult if you follow these steps.

- Now ask each half, as a group, to write down each step of the procedure *in order*. The students who saw the topic sentence (asterisk note) will do a much better job, with relative ease; the other half will struggle and probably fail.

- Then read or display to the entire class the sentence that the experimental group saw.

The experimental group saw a topic sentence for the targeted paragraph. As a result, their brains self-googled for information pertaining to doing the laundry and got ready to receive the steps in the process. Everything was interpreted accordingly, chunked, and networked into the existing background information (scripts and schemas) that the experimental group already had tucked away in their brains. Recall for them was easy.

The control group was absolutely unprepared for the information. The paragraph, obviously, is poorly written: the author purposely made vague references that, without the topic sentence, were relatively meaningless. Because the brains of the control group were not properly set up to interact with the information, they were not able to chunk or network the steps. As a result, their short-term memories overloaded with unrelated information, and data was lost.

Again, this is a contrived paragraph, purposely written to probe human memory. But it's a vivid demonstration of the power of a topic sentence (or thesis statement) to properly prepare readers for a message.

Transitions

Transitions, whether words, phrases, or entire sentences, tell readers what the relationship is between pieces of information. Knowing when transitions are needed is more of an art than a science: using too many of them sounds condescending or insulting; not providing them when needed results in confusion or misunderstanding. As we will see, the GUESS concept goes a long way toward making this rather mysterious decision more demonstrable.

Your students use transitions all the time when they speak. Further, they have seen them by the thousands, if not hundreds of thousands, in material they have read, both in your class and in their other content area classes. So the problem isn't so much that the concept of transitions is new to them. Two other problems await your assistance:

1. **Transition void.** Students may not see where transitions are needed. What they are writing makes perfect sense in their heads, so they keep going. But the reader is either blindsided or lost.

2. **Transition rut.** Students rely on a small handful of transitions, especially on the word *and*. They all too often stick in *and*, irrespective of the relationship between the two joined elements; this is sometimes referred to as *and-and writing*. If students use other transitions, they choose from a limited set rather than employing a variety of transitional devices.

Although there are no hard and fast rules to follow about the need for a transition, you can certainly demonstrate this requirement with the GUESS concept. Students can also move their writing up the stylistic ladder from childish to more mature by using transitions properly. The following demonstration illustrates both features.

Classroom Activity: Reconstructive Surgery

I tell my students that they are plastic surgeons. I refer to them as Dr. (Last Name or First Name) for the remainder of the exercise. I inform my doctors that they will be working with a patient who has been disfigured by a horrible accident: he has had his transitions amputated. Here is an example:

The following patient (The Patient after the Accident), an excerpt from a fifth-grade reading sample, arrives in the emergency room in pretty bad shape. Ask students to prepare for major surgery.

- **Diagnostic pass 1.** Have your students identify areas that will require future surgery—areas that contain GUESS errors.

- **Diagnostic pass 2.** Ask students to mark where the patient has been disfigured by writing that sounds childish or simplistic because transitions have been removed.

- **Reconstructive surgery.** Send the patient to the operating room. Ask the doctors to do reconstructive surgery, rewriting the passage to make it sound better (more sophisticated) and fixing the GUESS errors that they identified. (Optionally, you could provide students with a list of the transitions that are in the original to guide their reconstruction, as plastic surgeons might refer to a photograph.)

- **Postoperative analysis.** Contrast the original version with the patients that your doctors have repaired. Discuss the strengths and weaknesses of the various techniques and structures.

The Patient after the Accident

Dozens of Pacific green sea turtles are slowly gliding by me. I snorkel along a rugged reef. A snorkeler cuts me off. Another snorkeler cuts me off. "Hey!" I think. "Watch where you're going!"

Then, I realize: These aren't snorkelers. They're sea lions! The sea lions dart this way and that. The sea lions blow bubbles at me. The sea lions blow bubbles at the group I'm with. The sea lions bonk us on our backs. The sea lions swim off. The sea lions zoom back for more.

This is an excellent example of a passage that, stripped of its transitions, sounds childish. The first paragraph is missing a transition word—one little word ("suddenly") that makes the paragraph flow. The second paragraph contains six short sentences, all beginning with "The sea lions." The original passage, which follows, demonstrates several ways to avoid this common problem, including a participial phrase ("Darting this way and that"), a synonym, sentence combining, and even a dash. I would never expect my classes to actually come up with this exact solution, but attempting to do so creates lots of good discussions and teachable moments. Here is the original passage:

The Patient before the Accident

Dozens of Pacific green sea turtles are slowly gliding by me as I snorkel along a rugged reef. Suddenly, a snorkeler cuts me off. Then another. "Hey!" I think. "Watch where you're going!"

Then, I realize: These aren't snorkelers. They're sea lions! Darting this way and that, the creatures blow bubbles at me and the group I'm with. The sea lions bonk us on our backs and swim off—only to zoom back for more.

Here is another short example, this time targeting sentences that begin with "There is":

The Patient after the Accident

Humans aren't allowed to live on most of the Galápagos Islands. There is only one way you can experience this magical place. You must take a small motorboat called a *panga* to all the islands. There is no human threat. The animals are very friendly.

And here is the original:

The Patient before the Accident

Humans aren't allowed to live on most of the Galápagos Islands. In fact, the only way you can experience this magical place is by taking a small motorboat called a *panga* to all the islands. The lack of human threat makes the animals very friendly. (Gerosa)

In the original version, a transition phrase ("In fact") helps the reader connect the second sentence to the first. The paragraph also demonstrates two ways to rewrite sentences in order to remove the unnecessarily weak "There is" beginnings.

Exercises like this are pretty easy to create. Find a passage that is at or below the reading level of your class. Rewrite a couple of the paragraphs, stripping out all transition words, phrases, or sentences, and fixing any fragments or problem areas that may be created. Your new version should not contain any compound or complex sentences by definition—such sentences always require a transition word, punctuation, or phrase to tie them together. You now have a patient ready for some reconstructive surgery. You can target specific problem areas in your re-writes, as I have just done, or incorporate a variety of problems.

The first time you do this exercise, do it together as a class, modeling how you would think your way through the reconstruction. On subsequent exercises, gradually release control to the students, breaking the class into small groups or having students work individually.

Classroom Activity: Create a Patient

- Have your class find short excerpts that contain good examples of transitions.

- Ask students to create a patient by rewriting their selected passages, stripping them of their transitions, and giving you the stripped version.

- Think out loud in front of the class as you work to reconstruct a patient. Then compare your version with the original.

- Later, have students, individually or in small groups, create patients that they can exchange for reconstructive surgery. They can then contrast the fruits of their labor with the original passages, discussing strengths and weaknesses.

If you are working on a specific genre or rhetorical mode, this exercise is an excellent way to get students familiar with transitions that are commonly used in that type of writing. For example, the sample passage that I used in the reconstructive surgery activity is a narrative. This type of passage will contain transitions that pertain to time ordering—not exclusively, of course, but often. A process essay will contain process transitions, and so forth. You can ask your students to limit the passages they select to the specific genre or rhetorical mode that you are working with. This kind of exposure to transitions is far superior to simply giving students lists or tables of transitional devices from which to choose.

Paragraphing is also a transitional device, signaling a change of topics to readers. I will deal with this important device in Chapter 6.

Punctuation

When we speak, we send messages to our listeners in ways that add to the meaning contained in the words and sentence structures that we use. We can communicate by changing the intonation, changing the volume, using hand and arm gestures, changing our facial expressions, pausing, and so on. When we write, we have a much more limited set of tools, external to the language itself, with which to communicate: for the most part, all we have available are fonts and punctuation.

- **Fonts.** We can shout by WRITING IN ALL CAPS or emphasize by using bold, italics, or underlining. In the noncreative, nonpoetic world, that's about it.

- **Punctuation.** The primary purpose of punctuation is to help readers know where to chunk. (See Chapter 2 for an explanation of chunking.) The comma, period, question mark, and exclamation point carry the vast majority of the signaling load for chunking. Other punctuation marks, in addition to sending chunking signals, provide further information to readers about what comes next.

Fonts are not a problem for students to grasp. But punctuation can be problematic for student writers to master. Most students' reading brains master punctuation from a receptive perspective fairly quickly; mastering punctuation from a productive perspective requires more detailed exposure. The GUESS concept helps us to demonstrate the types of signals that punctuation marks send to the reader.

Classroom Demonstration: GUESS Signals
Let's examine punctuation marks by tapping into the reading brains of your students to help them determine what kinds of signals various punctuation marks send to the reader.

The comma. Most of the time, a comma is a clear signal to the reader to chunk. (For a detailed examination of the comma and chunking, see my book *Unleashing Your Language Wizards*.)

The period. A period is a neutral marker. All it tells the reader to do is to chunk the previous group of words as a completed unit—a sentence. You can demonstrate this to your classes easily by asking them to GUESS what comes next after a period. Show them a sentence such as the following, and ask them to help you make a list.

1. The accident was caused by smoke blowing onto the road. **[GUESS what is next]**

Several things could follow this period, including these:

- How the fire got started
- How many vehicles were involved, or how many people were hurt
- What the motorists should have done to prevent the accident
- What the rescue personnel did to help the injured
- What the weather was like, or how it hampered rescue operations
- What the terrain was like
- Nothing—this is the last sentence in the article

The period, then, is a straightforward device that simply tells the reader to chunk. It holds no promise for the future.[1]

The exclamation point. From a GUESS perspective, the exclamation point works exactly like the period: it holds no promise for the future. One could easily imagine a context in which each of the GUESSes we just listed could fit if sentence 1 ended in an exclamation point instead of a period. Instead of affecting what comes next in the text, the exclamation point affects what the reader has just processed: it signals strong emotion—surprise, shock, dismay, and so on—for the sentence it ends.

The question mark. A question mark is a signal to the reader to chunk, but it is decidedly not neutral. Your students have highly developed *speaking brains*, that is, knowledge about the inner workings of speech. Because speech contains a clear way to mark questions, most students readily grasp the purpose of the question mark. Contrasting the period GUESS with the question mark GUESS, however, is a great way to set the stage for GUESS explorations of more difficult punctuation marks. Here is how a question-mark GUESS discussion might look:

2. What caused the accident? **[GUESS what is next]**

Now the reader's GUESSes are severely limited. Notice how most of the GUESSes that fit sentence 1, in the previous discussion of periods, are nonsensical here. The GUESSes about the weather or terrain might fit, but only if they caused the accident. There are two viable options for what can come next:

- An answer to the question
- Another related question—perhaps one in a series of questions that, for the moment, are unanswered

The semicolon. With one minor exception,[2] a semicolon can always be replaced by a period; the opposite is not true at all. So, although the period sends a neutral signal to the reader's reading brain, the semicolon does not. The semicolon is a signal to chunk the previous group of words as a complete sentence; in addition, it shapes the reader's GUESS by telling her that the next sentence is going to be closely related to the one just finished. (The previous sentences of this paragraph illustrate this signaling device nicely. I could have used a period instead of a semicolon in both sentences, thereby sending no signal about the topic of the next sentence to you, my reader.) As the reader's brain is going through the rapid-fire process of interacting with the text, such a signal helps her make good GUESSes. That the occasional, correctly used semicolon contributes to the impression of sophisticated writing is a bonus.

The colon. The colon is also a clear signal to chunk the previous group of words. In fact, in the body of a formal piece of writing, the colon can be used only at the end of a complete sentence. In a formal writing context, then, the colon, like the period, is an unambiguous guide, telling the reader both *how* (end of sentence) and *where* (right here) to chunk. Like the semicolon, the colon is not neutral at all:

3a. Several things made the trip unpleasant. **[GUESS what is next]**

3b. Several things made the trip unpleasant: **[GUESS what is next]**

As we saw earlier, the period at the end of sentence 3a does not limit what comes next. After 3a, I could write about how I overcame or ignored the unpleasantries, how I could have avoided them, and so on. But the colon in sentence 3b severely limits the GUESS—a list of the things that made the trip unpleasant *must* come next. Note that the list does not have to contain more than one member:

3c. One thing made the trip unpleasant: the incessantly cold weather.

The colon, therefore, trumpets the following message to the reader: "Here's what I'm talking about."

The dash. As with almost all punctuation marks, the dash is a signal to chunk the previous group of words as a completed phrase or sentence. The reader's GUESS, though, is clearly constrained by the dash: it usually informs the reader that the writer is about to take a temporary side trip (sentence 4, which follows) or add another piece of information that is not of critical importance (sentence 5, which follows).

4. The information—later proven to be false—caused many people to use herbal supplements instead of prescribed medicine.

5. All of my homework—algebra, English, history, and biology—was destroyed by the fire.

Parentheses. Parentheses are similar to dashes, but they mark the information they enclose as even less important—added almost as an afterthought.

6. The additional features of the new printer (scan, fax, and copy) made it a very welcome addition to our office.

Punctuation Summary

Punctuation marks are substitutes for some of the nonverbal aspects of speech that are not available to the writer. Though virtually all punctuation marks are signals to the reader to chunk, their usage varies between absolutely required by rule and absolutely optional.

- Periods, exclamation points, and question marks are, for the most part, required by rule. Commas are often required also.
- The others—semicolon, colon, dash, parentheses—are stylistic choices that writers make. In addition, commas can be used stylistically for rhetorical effect.

Often, writers can use commas in place of dashes or parentheses. William Strunk and E. B. White note that a dash is "stronger than a comma, less formal than a colon, and more relaxed than parentheses" (9).

TABLE 3.1. Punctuation Overview

Punctuation	Chunking Signal	GUESS Message to Readers
Comma	End of phrase	GUESS a new item or phrase.
Period	End of sentence	GUESS a new sentence.
Question mark	End of sentence	GUESS the answer or another related question.
Exclamation point	End of sentence	Know that the sentence that just ended has high emotional content.
Semicolon	End of sentence	GUESS another sentence that is closely related to the previous one.
Colon	End of sentence (in formal writing)	GUESS a list (possibly of one item) that further exemplifies or explains.
Dash	End of phrase or sentence	GUESS a brief side trip or rather unimportant information.
Parentheses	End of phrase or sentence	GUESS extra, absolutely noncritical information.

Table 3.1 provides a summary of these punctuation marks, the kind of chunking that they signal, and the message that is sent to readers as they go through the sample-predict-confirm cycle.

Summary

This chapter showed how to apply the GUESS concept to several parts of a traditional essay.

- **Title.** A properly established title is the initial step in preparing the reader to process the contents by beginning the self-googling process. A demonstration of the power of a title was provided.
- **Introduction.** The most important function of an introduction is to allow the reader to GUESS the direction and, optionally, the general structure of an essay. Two ineffective introductions were analyzed, followed by one excellent example. These introductions allow student writers to experience the difference between being appropriately prepared as a reader to make good GUESSes and being unprepared.

- **Topic sentence or thesis statement.** A demonstration was provided showing how a topic sentence made the understanding and subsequent recall of the contents of a paragraph much easier. A good thesis statement offers the same functionality, but at the essay level instead of the paragraph level.
- **Transitions.** A classroom activity was given that showed what happens to a passage when it is rewritten without transitions. The activity gives students the opportunity to recreate the transitions.
- **Punctuation.** The primary function of punctuation is to show the reader where and how to chunk. The GUESS concept helps students to understand the signals that various punctuation marks send to readers.

Further Reading

For in-depth coverage of some of the earlier research exploring the effect of textual conventions on memory, see *Human Cognition* by John Bransford.

For details concerning punctuation in written English, see my book *Unleashing Your Language Wizards*.

Notes

1. The topic established by the sentence will, of course, limit GUESSes. It would make no sense, for example, for sentence 2 to discuss tsunamis, beef stew, or other unrelated topics. The period itself, however, isn't the limiting factor. Any sentence could follow sentence 1 and be mechanically correct.
2. A semicolon is used to separate the items in a series if any of the items within the series contains one or more commas.

4

Reading like Writers

Chapters 1–3 examined the processing that occurs in the reader's brain and how that processing relates to and affects writing. Now, let's change perspectives: we will peek inside the brains of student writers.

As students move up the grade ladder, they are exposed to ever-increasing amounts of professionally written and edited material from their subject area reading assignments. This kind of input is, from a brain-based perspective, "triple-X" rated:

- *Exposure:* processing a variety of well-written material across time creates . . .

- *Experience:* memory traces in areas of the brain that lie beyond conscious awareness that, in turn, are an excellent source for . . .

- *Exploration:* helping students to discover the receptive knowledge they have tucked away in their brains, and encouraging them to move it to the productive side.

In this and subsequent chapters, we'll look at some ways to take advantage of this triple-X-rated knowledge, that is, how to help student writers become aware of devices and techniques that professional authors use (and students readily understand when reading). This approach is a very effective way to raise student writing to the next level. If you involve your students in discovering writers' strategies, make it fun for them, and then celebrate rather than chastise their mistakes as they try out these new strategies in their own writing, three positive outcomes occur:

1. Students will begin to broaden their writing horizons by experimenting with structures that they already "know" when they read or hear them.

2. Students will see their writing improve without your having to rely on dry explanations and boring worksheets, an approach that most often does not transfer to student writing.

3. The gains students make will be durable instead of fleeting.

Analyzing Texts

If you truly want to help your students become better writers, if you truly want to prepare them for the academic, business, and professional writing challenges that lie in their future, then you must spend more time on the following:

- Helping students learn to read like writers. Help them learn to analyze readings, trying to get inside the minds of the authors to understand why they chose their words, structures, cohesive devices, paragraph structures, and so on. For example, how did the writer prepare readers so that they were ready to interact with the text? What did the writer do to ensure that readers would make good GUESSes? In other words, we must help students discover a writer's craft.

- Exploring how various elements affect the reading process and the reader's understanding of a passage, using a lot of "What if" analyses as you suggest various changes to the text.

Daniel Willingham, a cognitive psychologist who specializes in education, is the author of an excellent book—a must-read for teachers: *Why Don't Students Like School?* In one chapter, he highlights a clear, seemingly obvious result of research that we all too often lose sight of in the composition classroom: "Learning is influenced by many factors, but one factor trumps the others: students remember what they *think about*. That principle highlights the importance of getting students to *think about* the right thing at the right time" (p. 60; emphasis added). Elizabeth Hale applies Willingham's assertion to the composition classroom: "[W]hen you read like a writer, you ideally 'hang on' to what you see. Many, if not most, craft techniques are not out there on the surface for the taking. Reading like a writer . . . can excavate the craft that is embedded in the writing" (17). Rather than spend so much time *thinking about* plot, symbolism, character development, and so on, spend more time helping students *think about* what the writer did to make the text successful. If we want to teach our students to be better writers, we have to provide better ways for them to *think about* writing.

Every time we discuss a common reading, we should devote at least five to ten minutes to the analysis of some of the strategies that the author used in order to communicate her message clearly and effectively, taking into account the oft-neglected role of the reader's interaction with the text. Stuart Greene affirms that "an emphasis on the mindful study of texts, either through imitation or immersion, is of value, but these approaches have tended to neglect the active role readers play in constructing meaning in both comprehending and composing" (35).

We should help students to discover these strategies using a gradual release of control approach, described in Chapter 1. The following classroom activities will provide you with a variety of ways to help student writers *think about* how professional writers write—in ways that students genuinely enjoy.

Classroom Activity: Mining Texts

The term *mining texts* refers to the careful dissection of a text, looking closely at the strategies the author used to make it work. Greene puts it this way: "Whereas teachers often encourage a critical reading of individual texts as an end in itself, mining is part of an ongoing effort to learn specific rhetorical and linguistic devices" (36). Mining texts is especially important for today's students because most of them read less professionally written material for pleasure than did students of past generations, so they are denied the benefits of this increased exposure to good writing.

Begin the mining process by modeling it several times for or with your class. Once students get the hang of it, they can, with gentle guidance, take over the responsibility. To illustrate, let's work through an example. Imagine that the class has read Maya Angelou's "New Directions."[1] Let's limit ourselves to the opening three paragraphs, which follow, for this example.

An excellent way of mining a text is to divide students into groups, assigning each group specific tasks. Although I am creating specific groups for this example, the number of groups and the tasks assigned can vary according to the ability of the students and your lesson plans—past, present, and future. Here are the groups that I might create:

1. **Introduction group.** How does the author present background information that prepares the reader to make good GUESSes? What information is absolutely critical for the reader, and what information is included to add flavor or to make the writing more interesting? (If we were mining the entire short story, I might ask this group to closely examine the conclusion to see how the author wraps things up.)

2. **Transitions group.** How does the author connect the information in these paragraphs? Specifically, what words, phrases, and punctuation does the author use to help the reader process the content and to prevent GUESS errors? Note any examples of parallel structures that you find. (If we were mining the entire story, I would assign sections of the story to different transitions groups.)

3. **Language group.** How does the author create variety in her language structure? What if some sentences were written differently? How does the language help you to identify the author's or character's voice? (If we were mining the entire story, I would assign sections of the story to different language groups.)

Here are the three paragraphs. To save space, I have underlined some of the transition devices and highlighted the parallel structures that I might help students in the transitions group to identify.

> In 1903 the late Mrs. Annie Johnson of Arkansas found herself with two toddling sons, very little money, a slight ability to read and add simple numbers. To this picture add a disastrous marriage and the burdensome fact that Mrs. Johnson was a Negro.
>
> When she told her husband, Mr. William Johnson, of her dissatisfaction with their marriage, he conceded that he too found it to be less than he expected and had been secretly hoping to leave and study religion. He added that he thought God was calling him not only to preach but to do so in Enid, Oklahoma. He did not tell her that he knew a minister in Enid with whom he could study and who had a friendly, unmarried daughter. They parted amicably, Annie keeping the one-room house and William taking most of the cash to carry himself to Oklahoma.
>
> Annie, over six feet tall, big-boned, decided that she would not go to work as a domestic and leave her "precious babes" to anyone else's care. There was no possibility of being hired at the town's cotton gin or lumber mill, but maybe there was a way to make the two factories work for her. In her words, "I looked up the road I was going and back the way I come, and since I wasn't satisfied, I decided to step off the road and cut me a new path." She told herself that she wasn't a fancy cook but that she could "mix groceries well enough to scare hunger away from a starving man (19)."

I could easily write an entire chapter examining the beauty, cohesiveness, and rich language choices contained in these three paragraphs. I'll just hit some of the key points for the three student groups:

Introduction group. All three of these paragraphs are presented as background information to set up Angelou's story, each with its own role to play.

- The first paragraph describes Annie's situation at the beginning of the story.
- The second paragraph briefly outlines how Annie came to be in that condition.
- The third paragraph shows Annie's thought processes as she struggles to find a solution to her dilemma. The rest of the story deals with her solution.

In order to know what information is critical for the readers, one would, of course, have to read the entire short story. That Annie's marriage fell apart is certainly crucial background information; the details of her husband's "calling" could, from a purely factual perspective, be omitted, but this certainly adds interest and flavor to the story. Further, Angelou's brief description of Annie in paragraph 3 is not absolutely required information, but . . . .

Transition group. See the underlined and shaded areas, being sure to point out how some of the commas help the reader see where one point ends and the next begins. Also note that each new paragraph is an important signal to the reader that a new (but related) topic is coming.

Language group. This group needs the most assistance. The students need to develop a sharp eye for things the author did with her language choices, and they need to ask a lot of "What if" questions.

Let's briefly mine each paragraph.

- Paragraph 1
  - The first sentence has a parallel series, without "and" before the last item. Why did Angelou omit "and"? What if "and" were inserted in the series? What effect would it have?
  - What if Angelou had begun the last sentence with "She had a disastrous marriage . . ." instead of "To this picture add . . ."? Why did she write it the way she did?
  - Words like "toddling," "disastrous," and "burdensome" help create the voice of an educated storyteller writing for adults.
- Paragraph 2
  - What if the first sentence were written as three separate sentences? "She told her husband, Mr. William Johnson, of her dissatisfaction

with their marriage. He conceded that he too found it to be less than he expected. He had been secretly hoping to leave and study religion." Which version do you prefer, and why?

- In the second sentence, Angelou uses "not only to . . . but to . . . ." What if this sentence were written as follows? "He added that God was calling him to preach in Enid, Oklahoma." Which version do you prefer, and why?

- What if the last sentence were written as three sentences? "They parted amicably. Annie kept the one-room house. William took most of the cash to carry himself to Oklahoma." Which version do you prefer, and why?

• Paragraph 3

- What if the first sentence were written as follows? "Annie was over six feet tall, and she had big bones. She decided that . . . ." Why do you think Angelou decided to structure the sentence differently? What effect does her sentence structure have on the reader?

- Why did Angelou put quotes around "precious babes"?

- Why did Angelou decide to quote Annie in this paragraph? What does Annie's language help the reader to understand about her?

Mining common readings is a great way to bring otherwise unexamined details to student writers' conscious attention—to get them to *think about* it. Doing so, in combination with some of the other activities in this chapter, will help students develop strategies for a more sophisticated style through an osmosis-like process, rather than attempting to implant these strategies using memorization and drills. As Willingham notes, "[Y]our memory is not a product of what you want to remember or what you try to remember; it's a product of what you *think about*" (p. 41, emphasis added).

Classroom Application: Text-Mining Competition
Once students become comfortable with this type of activity, divide them into groups and have them compete with each other.

- **Transitions.** Ask students, "Who can find the most transition devices in a given passage?"
- **"What if" Q&A.** Have each group write "What if" questions such as the ones I modeled in the previous activity. You serve as the judge, Olympics style. Hold up a card with a number from one to ten, judging the quality

of the questions. The more interesting the technique or structure students select to "What if," the higher the score. (If, for example, one group took a compound sentence joined by "and," and then "What-if"'d it into two simple sentences, the group would not score very highly.) Then ask the other group to respond to the question, and judge the answer similarly. Your explanations of why you assigned the numbers to each group can lead to interesting discussions and help focus the students on craft that would otherwise go totally unnoticed.

• **Comma quiz.** Commas always seem to befuddle students. You and I "feel" commas—our experience with reading and writing has helped us develop an automatic pilot for most comma decisions. Students lack this automaticity. Memorizing rules and doing worksheets serves as a suitable beginning step for our students, but these activities won't make much of a contribution to the development of comma automaticity. In contrast, mining texts for comma information, especially in a competitive atmosphere, is an excellent way to build comma skills. Here is the simple procedure:

1. Group A finds a comma (or matching pair of commas) in a targeted passage, and then asks Group B to explain why it is (or they are) there.

2. If Group B's explanation satisfies you, that group gets the point. If Group B fails, Group A can earn the point by providing an alternate explanation.

3. The two groups then change positions, taking turns asking and explaining until the game is over.

When doing this activity, be sure to keep in mind that there are two kinds of commas: those required by rule, which I call *head commas*, and those placed for rhetorical effect, which I call *heart commas*. If, during this activity, one group queries the other group about a heart comma (one that is optional), and the other group identifies it as such, then that group is awarded the point. But if the comma is indeed required by rule, the point is not awarded unless the original group can explain the rule.

• **Sentence beginners.** Research shows that 25 to 33 percent of the sentences in a professionally written piece begin with something other than the subject phrase (Christensen and Christensen, and Schuster, respectively). I call these non-subject-phrase structures *sentence beginners*.[2] In contrast, inexperienced or weak student writers tend to start almost every sentence with the subject phrase.

1. Have one group find a sentence in the passage that has a sentence beginner.

2. Ask the other group to explain why the author decided to use that specific sentence beginner there and, optionally, how that sentence beginner could be moved to another position or made into its own sentence.

3. Then switch assignments. Continue until all sentence beginners have been identified and discussed, awarding points accordingly.

Classroom Application: Text-Mining Logs

Have students keep a text-mining journal or log. Once you have mined a short passage for writer's craft, give students a few minutes to add their favorite sentence or technique from that passage to their logs. Each entry should have three parts:

1. **Source.** Have students write the exact source (a good way to practice citing sources if doing so is part of your teaching agenda). At a minimum, they should record the author, title, and page number of the sentence so that they can go back to it if they need to see it again in context.

2. **Sentence.** Ask students to copy the sentence(s), word for word.

3. **Analysis.** Have students give a brief overview of the context for the sentence and what appealed to them.

Then, before students begin to write something on their own, or as they are revising a rough draft, have them read through their logs to get ideas that they might be able to use in their essays. (We will explore more sentence-level mining activities in Chapter 5.)

Classroom Activity: Says–Does

This activity comes from pages 65–68 of *Strategic Writing*, an excellent book by Deborah Dean. Here's how it works: Take a passage from a common reading that you are discussing with the class, and break it into logical chunks. Often, each paragraph would be one chunk, but in a passage with especially short paragraphs or dialogue, you might want to combine some of them. For simplicity's sake, I will assume that each chunk is a paragraph. Make two passes through the passage:

1. **Says.** Ask individual students to tell you what each paragraph says—a good way to build summarizing skills. Allow each student a moment to look over the paragraph if necessary, but ask them to give the summary without referring to it.

2. **Does.** Now ask students to tell you what each paragraph does—what role it plays, what purpose it serves, how it affects the reader. During this phase, students should ignore the paragraph's content, focusing instead on its function in the overall flow of the text. Ask students to show you specific language that contributes to the paragraph's effect on the reader: transitions, imagery, specific structures, metaphors or similes, word choices that evoke certain emotions, and so on. Don't let students drift back into the specific details of each paragraph; their job now is to see how each paragraph moves things forward, and to try to discover devices that the author used to make that movement smooth, effective, and properly emotional. (I gave a brief example of "Does" in the discussion immediately following the earlier Angelou excerpt.)

Asking students to view passages as contributors to the overall flow of a piece of writing is a great way to expose them to a writer's craft. As Dean puts it, "In discovering what the text does, students are also discovering how it does it, how language and sentence fluency help to create the effects they feel" (*Strategic Writing* 67). This type of exposure will help student writers broaden their writing horizons, acquiring new structures, techniques, and word choices that will help them develop a more mature, effective writing style.

Classroom Activity: Writing Logs

Another good suggestion from Dean is for student writers to create writing logs, similar to what I suggested earlier when discussing mining text, but targeting a wide variety of sources (*Strategic Writing* 17–19). Dean proposes that teachers have students create entries for their writing logs based on their own reading experience instead of on common readings. (Dean recommends that they turn in fifteen entries every three weeks or so, but my experience has been that five to ten entries is a more reasonable goal.)

Each entry consists of four parts: (1) the source, (2) the passage of interest, (3) what works, and (4) how you might use it. I model the activity for my students (as does Dean), and then it's up to the students. They draw on any written source: content area readings (excluding anything we have mined in our class; they need to discover these items on their own), things they are reading for pleasure, emails, blogs, instructions—anything they happen to read. I instruct them to constantly be on the lookout for effective sentences that contain interesting structures, punctuation, word usage, imagery, and so on.

The assignment is automatic: every third Friday, my students know that they must hand in their writing logs with their new entries in place. Here is one of the models that I give to my students:

Source: "Mother Tongue" by Amy Tan, page 29.

Passage: "You should know that my mother's expressive command of English belies how much she actually understands. She reads the *Forbes* report, listens to *Wall Street Week*, converses daily with her stockbroker, reads all of Shirley MacLaine's books with ease—all kinds of things I can't begin to understand."

What Works: The author uses a series of specific examples, but she doesn't use "and" before the last item. Instead, she uses a dash and gives a more general summary of the things her mother can handle in English.

Using It: Any time I want to show a selected set of examples of what I am talking about, this is a great way to do it. I can list a few of them, ending the series with a dash and a summary of what I am referring to. I like this as a substitute for when I want to end a series with "and so on."[3]

Here is an example at the word level. One of my students chose the first sentence of Tan's passage because he was taken by the word *belies*. He wrote the following:

I've never seen this word before. This sounds so much better than saying things like "You would never know how much English my mother understands by listening to her talk" or "Listening to her talk hides how much she can understand." Tan's use of this word makes her sound more educated. It's an amazing word.

And sure enough, later on in the semester, up popped this word in one of this student's essays. I'm not saying that everything your students put into their writing logs will appear in their writing—far from it. But this type of activity is at least some exposure, an invitation to try new ways of expressing themselves.

At the beginning of this chapter, I quoted Willingham, who noted that the single most important factor in learning is that "students remember what they think about." The writing log is a good way to get students to truly think about how a variety of writers express their messages, and to consider how they might apply some of these same techniques to their own writing.

You may have a few students in every class who don't get it at first. This is such a totally new way of approaching the reading of a text that it takes some repetition before they get the hang of it. But I've never had a student who didn't catch on after a misstep or two.

Be sure to have your students reread their logs before they write or revise their writing. And tell them that if they try something new and don't quite get it right, this type of "error" is a *good* thing: natural human learning is a trial-and-error process. Let students know that this won't hurt their grade, and that you will help them get it right next time. In fact, before they submit a paper for a final grade, I encourage students to ask me questions about new things they are trying from their logs. I help them get it right before they hand in the paper.

Audience

In Chapter 2 we saw how the GUESS concept helped students become more aware of what readers bring with them into the reading process and how that knowledge should affect what we write. Dean sums things up nicely: "Thinking about audience has an impact on ideas (which ones I choose and which I leave out); organization (what should come first, second, last); language (what words I use and how I use them); even genre (whether I should use a memo or a letter form)" (*Strategic Writing* 84).

Students will do a much better job of taking audience into account once they are aware of some of the components of good writing that combine to tailor the content to different groups of people. Research indicates that, at an amazingly early age, students already have a subconscious feel for when a text is suitable for a specific audience. Mark Overmeyer provides a vivid demonstration of this phenomenon. He recounts an incident with first graders: before reading a book to them, he asked students to tell him if he was reading it incorrectly. Rather than reading the actual story, he made a comment about the illustration on each page: "I see owls." "I hear frogs." Here is how he describes what happened next:

> One girl interrupted my "reading" and said, "That's wrong."
>
> "How do you know?" I asked. "My words match the pictures on the page. How do you know that what I said is not what Cynthia Rylant wrote?"
>
> "Because who would buy a book like that?" she asked.
>
> Who indeed. And a six-year-old just demonstrated that she knows that writers can use language to delight, not just to inform. (20)

In other words, this first grader *knew* that the content that Overmeyer delivered was not suitable for the reading audience for whom the book was intended.

The next demonstration is designed to help students become more aware of this subconscious (that is, receptive) knowledge so that they can apply it consciously when writing.

Classroom Activity: GUESS the Audience
Select a paragraph for analysis. Have students read it and complete the following questionnaire. When students have finished, discuss their answers.

GUESS the Audience Questionnaire

1. What age group did the writer have in mind?

   a. Children b. Teens c. Adults

   What words or sentences lead you to this conclusion?

2. What is the educational level of the intended audience?

   a. Elementary b. Secondary c. General d. Specialist

   If the anticipated educational level were different, what words or sentences might the author have to change?

3. What background or experience does the writer assume on the part of the reader?

   a. None b. Minimal c. Average d. In-depth

   What parts of the paragraph influenced your answer?

4. What need(s) or interest(s) is the author trying to meet?

   a. Explain b. Persuade c. Inform d. Entertain e. Other _____

   Why do you think so?

5. What kind of self-image is the author trying to project to readers? What parts of the paragraph influenced your answer?

Learning to Write for Readers: Using Brain-Based Strategies by John T. Crow © 2011 NCTE.

Following are four sample paragraphs taken from different sources. I have chosen these paragraphs because I know that you, my intended audience, can handle them. Your choice of paragraphs to analyze will depend, of course, on the level of the students in your class and the types of writing you want to cover. As you read the following paragraphs, think about how you might respond to the questionnaire.

1. Fisher Willow, a headstrong young heiress, chafes under the constraints of proper Southern society and rebels by asking the impoverished but handsome son of her father's caretaker, Jimmy Dobyne, to escort her to the major Memphis social events of the season. The relationship is purely a business arrangement at the outset, with Fisher paying for Jimmy's time and attention, but when she discovers that she really loves him, she finds it impossible to re-write the rules and earn the affection she tried to buy. (Rev. of *The Loss of a Teardrop Diamond*)

2. For such a foul-tempered, ferocious and smelly creature, the Tasmanian devil is beloved in its native Australia, where it is considered a symbol of the country's frontier roughness. (The dog-sized marsupial's second life as a Looney Tunes character hasn't hurt its popularity either.) But as fierce as it is, the devil—which is found only in the Australian island-state of Tasmania—is in danger of going extinct. (Walsh)

3. It has six legs, two pairs for each part of the thorax (the central part of the insect that the head, wings, and legs are attached to), and an exoskeleton, which is an outer shell. It may also have two pairs of wings, two sets of jaws, and two kinds of eyes. What is this creature? It is a typical insect, and insects of all kinds have existed on earth for millions of years. Sometimes we think of all insects as pests. Human life, however, would have a difficult time continuing without insects, because they pollinate plants and are a food source for many animals. Besides, insects, especially the social ones, are fascinating. ("Social Insects")

4. It was the Dover road that lay, on a Friday night late in November, before the first of the persons with whom this history has business. The Dover Road lay, as to him, beyond the Dover mail, as it lumbered up Shooter's Hill. He walked uphill in the mire by the side of the mail, as the rest of the passengers did; not because they had the least relish for walking exercise, under the circumstances, but because the hill, and the harness, and the mud, and the mail, were all so heavy, that the horses had three times already come

to a stop, besides once drawing the coach across the road, with the mutinous intent of taking it back to Blackheath. Reins and whips and coachman and guard, however, in combination, had read that article of war which forbade a purpose otherwise strongly in favour of the argument, that some brute animals are endued with Reason; and the team had capitulated and returned to its duty. (Dickens 6)

Next is the source for each of the preceding paragraphs. That information should suffice to allow you to see how your audience expectations conform with the authors' reality.

1. Summary of a movie plot taken from a website that accumulates movie reviews
2. Introductory paragraph to a *Time* article titled "Decoding the Tasmanian Devil's Deadly Cancer"
3. Excerpt from a fourth-grade reading selection in the Florida Comprehensive Assessment Test
4. Selection from the Charles Dickens classic *A Tale of Two Cities*

The rich classroom discussions that typically follow analyses of this nature will help make your students more consciously aware of the importance of audience and of the components of good writing that combine to meet their needs. As an added bonus, the discussions will provide some interesting insights into how your students view a piece of writing.

Classroom Activity: Change the Audience

As a follow-up activity, you can ask your students to rewrite a paragraph for a different audience, much as we discussed in Chapter 2. You could, for example, ask them to rewrite the passage we examined about insects for an older, more knowledgeable audience, or rewrite the Dickens passage for their friends' reading and entertainment.

Classroom Activity: Contrast the Audience

Whereas the activity "GUESS the Audience" involves analyzing writings that have nothing in common with each other, this exercise involves analyzing two or more paragraphs that deal with the same topic, but were clearly intended for different audiences. This type of activity provides a clear demonstration of the fact that audience influences virtually every aspect of writing. In this exercise, tell the students in advance the source and the intended audience. Then have them fill out a Textual Analysis Worksheet (see Appendix B for a blank worksheet) for each, modeling the process at first and then gradually turning it over to them.

To illustrate this activity, examine the following three passages and Figures 4.1–4.3, all of which deal with the recent discovery of the function of the human appendix. Figures 4.1–4.3 are completed worksheets you can use to model this activity with your students.

What the Appendix Is Good For

Emily Sohn, *Science News for Kids*

Throughout history, scientists, too, have wondered about structures that don't seem to do anything useful. The appendix is a popular example. This little, worm-like pouch is about four inches long and less than half an inch wide.

The organ grows near where the long intestine meets the short intestine. The intestines are essential for digestion, but the appendix appears to just sit there.

"It's a dead-end sack," says William Parker, an immunologist at Duke University in Durham, N.C. "It doesn't go anywhere."

Parker didn't start out intending to study the appendix. His specialty is the immune system—a collection of organs, cells and molecules that our bodies use to stay healthy. But his research led him to the appendix anyway.

Parker knew that the human body is full of tiny organisms called bacteria, which can overwhelm the immune system, cause infections and make a person sick. He also knew that some bacteria are good for human health. Among other benefits, these "good" bacteria help people digest food and fight off "bad" bacteria that cause disease.

Scientists Discover True Function of Appendix Organ

Barbara Miller, *ABC News*

Scientists say the appendix might have been a place for good bacteria to localize in, like a little cul-de-sac away from everything else.

It has long been regarded as a potentially troublesome, redundant organ, but American researchers say they have discovered the true function of the appendix.

The researchers say it acts as a safe house for good bacteria, which can be used to effectively reboot the gut following a bout of dysentery or cholera.

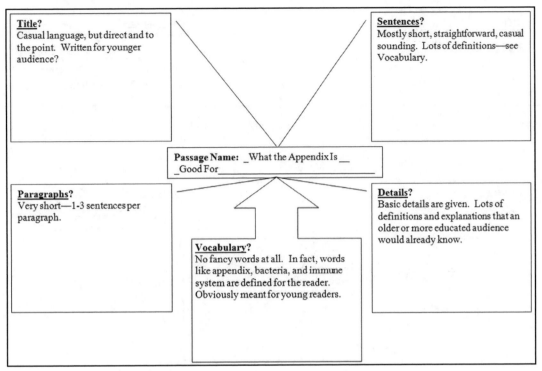

FIGURE 4.1. What the appendix is good for.

The conventional wisdom is that the small pouch protruding from the first part of the large intestine is redundant and many people have their appendix removed and appear none the worse for it.

Scientists from the Duke University Medical Centre in North Carolina say following a severe bout of cholera or dysentery, which can purge the gut of bacteria essential for digestion, the reserve good bacteria emerge from the appendix to take up the role.

But Professor Bill Parker says the finding does not mean we should cling onto our appendices at all costs.

"It's very important for people to understand that if their appendix gets inflamed, just because it has a function it does not mean they should try to keep it in," he said.

"So it's sort of a fun thing that we've found, but we don't want it to cause any harm, we don't want people to say, 'oh, my appendix has a function,' so I'm not going to go to the doctor, I'm going to try to hang onto it."

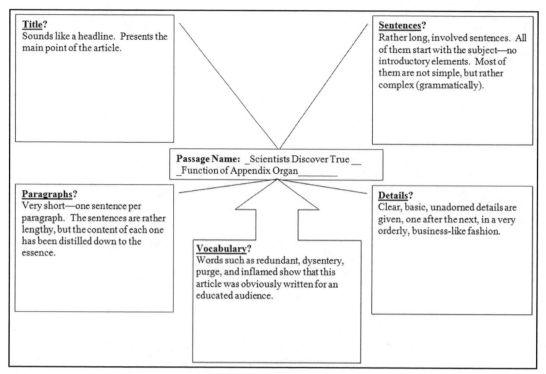

Title?
Sounds like a headline. Presents the main point of the article.

Sentences?
Rather long, involved sentences. All of them start with the subject—no introductory elements. Most of them are not simple, but rather complex (grammatically).

Passage Name: _Scientists Discover True_
_Function of Appendix Organ_____

Paragraphs?
Very short—one sentence per paragraph. The sentences are rather lengthy, but the content of each one has been distilled down to the essence.

Details?
Clear, basic, unadorned details are given, one after the next, in a very orderly, business-like fashion.

Vocabulary?
Words such as redundant, dysentery, purge, and inflamed show that this article was obviously written for an educated audience.

FIGURE 4.2. Scientists discover true function.

Biofilms in the Large Bowel Suggest an Apparent Function of the Human Vermiform Appendix

R. Randall Bollinger, et al., *Journal of Theoretical Biology*

The observations described above, in conjunction with the survival advantages afforded to bacteria by biofilms (Costerton, 1995, 1999; Costerton et al., 1995) and the architecture of the human large bowel, give rise to the idea that the appendix is a compartment well suited for maintaining beneficial or commensal microorganisms, being well positioned to avoid contamination by pathogenic organisms present transiently in the fecal stream. Indeed, the narrow lumen of the appendix as well as its location at the lower end of the cecum are both factors that afford relative protection from the fecal stream as it is propelled by peristalsis. Given the metabolic advantages (Bradshaw et al., 1994, 1997) and other advantages (Costerton, 1995, 1999; Costerton et al., 1995) that biofilms are known to afford bacteria, biofilm formation in the appendix is expected to be a relatively effective means of preserving and protecting commensal bacteria. In essence, the structure of the appendix is expected to enhance the protective effect of biofilm formation for commensal bacteria. Effective biofilm formation by commensal bacte-

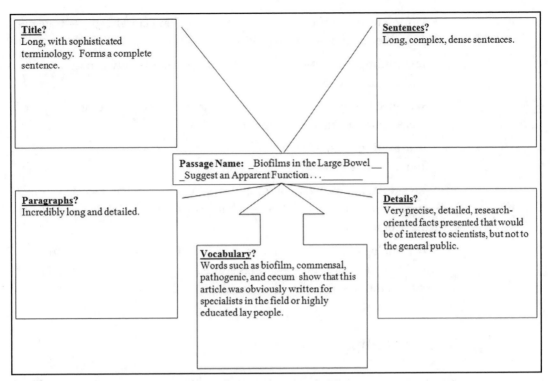

Title?
Long, with sophisticated terminology. Forms a complete sentence.

Sentences?
Long, complex, dense sentences.

Passage Name: _Biofilms in the Large Bowel_ _Suggest an Apparent Function . . ._____

Paragraphs?
Incredibly long and detailed.

Details?
Very precise, detailed, research-oriented facts presented that would be of interest to scientists, but not to the general public.

Vocabulary?
Words such as biofilm, commensal, pathogenic, and cecum show that this article was obviously written for specialists in the field or highly educated lay people.

FIGURE 4.3. Biofilms.

ria in the appendix is expected to facilitate not only the exclusion of pathogens, but also the adherence of the nonpathogenic commensal organisms within that cavity. Regular shedding and regeneration of biofilms within the appendix would be expected to re-inoculate the large bowel with commensal organisms in the event that the large bowel became infected by a pathogen and was flushed out as a defensive response to that infection. (829)

Summary

This chapter explored classroom activities to help students learn to read like writers.

- **Triple-X rated:** awareness that *exposure* to well-written material creates *experience*—memory traces in one's subconscious—that is rich ground for *exploration*.

- **Mining texts:** carefully dissecting a text, looking closely at the strategies the author employed to make it work.
- **Text-mining competitions:** ways to set up contests between groups of students as they mine texts.
- **Sentence beginners:** introductory elements—something other than the subject phrase—that start sentences.
- **Text-mining logs:** building a collection of writer's craft and strategies from mined texts.
- **Says-does:** analyzing a paragraph, looking first at what it says (a summary of its content) and then at what it does (its function in the flow of the overall text).
- **Writing logs:** collections similar to text-mining logs, but created from a wide variety of sources—things students read in their everyday life outside the classroom and have analyzed individually.

Further Reading

For in-depth explorations into dissecting writing to see what makes it work, see *Crafting Writers, K–6* by Elizabeth Hale and *Strategic Writing* by Deborah Dean.

Notes

1. The entire short story is available at http://www.nexuslearning.net/books/Holt_ElementsofLit-3/Collection%204/new%20directions.htm.

2. In our targeted passage, two of the nine sentences contain sentence beginners: "When she told her husband" and "In her words." I do not count "There was" as a true sentence beginner. See my book *Unleashing Your Language Wizards* for a detailed examination of sentence beginners, interrupters, and expanders.

3. When I originally wrote the next-to-last sentence of the first paragraph of this section, I ended it with "and so on." As I revised this chapter, this structure was fresh in my mind, so I changed it to its current form. This kind of behavior is exactly what I hope writing logs instill in my students.

Exploring the Concept of Sentence

I n a *New York Times* editorial titled "Devoid of Content," Stanley Fish opined that "millions of American college and high school students will stride across the stage, take diploma in hand and set out to the wider world, most of them utterly unable to write a clear and coherent English sentence. How is this possible? The answer is simple and even obvious: Students can't write clean English sentences because they are not being taught what sentences are."

Although I am usually in total agreement with Fish's ideas and opinions, I have to take exception to this one. Upon close analysis, the concept of *sentence* is a very slippery thing to pin down. We will start this chapter with demonstrations and activities to get students thinking about the concept of sentence, to allow them to see how difficult it is to define, and then to provide ways to explore their inner sense of this concept.

Whether or not we can define them, sentences are indisputably the building blocks of any piece of writing. And, of course, there is much to be learned from the sentences that professional authors use. So we will devote a portion of this chapter to ways for students to learn about sentences from the masters.

While it's true that sentences are building blocks, they can't function as such unless they interlock with each other. Failure to do so is an easy way to create GUESS errors. We will, therefore, devote the remainder of this chapter to an examination of how sentences interrelate to make a piece of writing cohesive.

What Is a Sentence?

The best way to examine the concept of sentence is to, once again, tap into the subconscious knowledge that your students have tucked away in their speaking and reading brains. The following demonstrations show how I explore students' existing concept of sentence as we try to build a working definition of the concept.

Classroom Demonstration: An Inadequate Definition of *Sentence*

We all talk about sentences a lot—as if we knew exactly what they are and why they are important. You have read, written, heard, and spoken countless thousands of sentences—but do you truly know what a sentence is?

Let's start with a definition of a sentence that needs some serious work:

Definition 1. A sentence is a structure that *begins with a capital letter and ends with a period (or exclamation point or question mark).*

1. *According to definition 1*, is the following a sentence?

   Example 1. Under.

2. According to *your* understanding, is example 1 a sentence?

3. *According to definition 1*, is the following a sentence?

   Example 2. Under the bed.

4. According to *your* understanding, is example 2 a sentence?

5. What do you think is missing from both of these examples?

You may not be able to state exactly what a sentence *is*, but you certainly know what it *is not*. Although examples 1 and 2 are sentences according to our working definition, neither one matches your understanding of the concept of sentence. Clearly, our definition needs some work.

Definition 2. A sentence is *a complete thought*. It begins with a capital letter and ends with a period (or exclamation point or question mark).

1. *According to definition 2*, is the following a sentence?

   Example 1. Under the bed.

2. Imagine the following conversation. *According to definition 2*, is the last part of the conversation a sentence?

   Example 2. Speaker A: "Where did you put my shoes?" Speaker B: "Under the bed."

3. Example 1 clearly is *not* a sentence, yet the *same words* coming out of Speaker B's mouth in example 2 seem perfectly fine. What's the difference between the two?

The idea of a sentence being a complete thought doesn't appear to work very well. When the expression "under the bed" is written by itself, the words are an incomplete thought. Yet when said in response to Speaker A's question, these same words seem complete. If the same three words can be perceived as a complete thought in one instance and an incomplete thought in another, then we still need to work on our definition. Let's briefly examine *why* example 1 (definition 2) seems very wrong, yet example 2 seems just fine.

- In example 1, the words come out of nowhere. The phrase is not connected to anything, so it makes no sense.

- In example 2, the phrase is said in response to Speaker A's question. Both speakers understand exactly what Speaker B means: "(*I put your shoes*) Under the bed." When speaking, there is often no need to repeat information that has already been established, so these kinds of omissions are commonplace.

If we were allowed to write exactly as we speak, then we wouldn't need to *learn* how to write—we could simply write down our thoughts as if we were saying them. Unfortunately, writing is *not* frozen speech. When we write, we normally do not have two or more people bouncing ideas back and forth. The reader has to be able to understand what we mean *without the writer being there*. This fact causes some rules to change. Let's return to our "complete thought" definition for some further exploration.

Definition 2. *(continued)*

4. How many complete thoughts are expressed in each of the following examples?

a. I continued to walk. However, my feet hurt. ____

b. I continued to walk even though my feet hurt. ____

c. Even though my feet hurt. ____

Again we see that the "complete thought" definition has problems. "My feet hurt" is clearly a complete thought. In 4a, it retains this characteristic. But in 4b, what appears to be two complete thoughts are treated as one complete sentence—or one complete thought, according to our definition. To make matters worse, in 4c, the same concept is no longer considered to be a sentence—so is it therefore no longer a complete thought? This "complete thought" concept is not working at all. Let's try a different approach.

> **Definition 3.** A sentence is *a group of words that shows someone or something doing something.* It begins with a capital letter and ends with a period (or exclamation point or question mark).
>
> 1. *According to definition 3,* is the following a sentence? Why or why not?
>
>   **Example 1.** Under the bed.
>
> 2. *According to definition 3,* is the following a sentence? Why or why not?
>
>   **Example 2.** I put your shoes under the bed.
>
> 3. *According to definition 3,* is the following a sentence? Why or why not?
>
>   **Example 3.** Mistakes were made.

Definition 3 is certainly an improvement. It clearly rules out example 1: this phrase does not state *who* does something, nor does it state *what* is done. Example 3, however, shows that the definition isn't perfect. It does not state *who* made the mistakes. Yet it feels like—and is—a complete sentence.

What have we learned through our explorations so far? Defining a sentence is difficult! That's the bad news. The good news is that, even though we can't seem to be able to define the concept of sentence, we already have a pretty good feel for what it is. This next activity will take full advantage of that insight.

Classroom Activity: Five Words in a Sentence

The same Stanley Fish, whose opinion I disagreed with at the beginning of this chapter, suggested an exercise that demonstrates what students already know about sentences:

- Pick five words more or less at random, mixing in a variety of parts of speech, and present them to your class. Ask students—individually or in small groups—to meaningfully incorporate all five words into a single sentence. Let's use *guitar, chair, beautifully, outrageous,* and *milk* for our example. (I say "meaningfully" to prohibit silliness such as "Our teacher asked us to use guitar, chair, beautifully, outrageous, and milk in a sentence.") You will, of course, get a wide variety of sentences. Here is one possibility:

    A **beautifully** trained professional who can sit in a **chair** and play **outrageous guitar** for hours might want a glass of **milk** when she is finished.

- Ask students what they did in order to transform five unrelated words into a meaningful sentence. They will struggle to put into words how they accomplished this task. Then ask them questions such as the following:

1. How do you know who did what to whom or with what?
2. What is the role of each of the five target words in your sentences?
3. Can any of the five target words be interchanged with each other?
4. Can any words or groups of words be moved to a different position without changing the meaning?

What you are trying to get students to come up with is something like this: "We added more words and put all of these words together in a certain order so that they interacted with each other in a meaningful way." In other words, the words formed relationships with each other. What students undoubtedly won't say is that these relationships were captured in a coded system we call English grammar. So students are talking about English grammar when they answer the questions in this activity, whether they realize it or not. And because they were able to perform the task, they most certainly have some internal grasp of the concept of sentence.

Sentence Gathering

As we discussed in earlier chapters, students are able to read, understand, and even produce sentences that they might never think to use in their writing. I will present two ways of mining writing for interesting sentences, one building on the other. The goal for these two activities is the same: to help students integrate a variety of sentence structures into their writing by making them consciously aware of structures that their reading brains process effortlessly at a subconscious level, but that they may not incorporate into their writing. The objective here is *not* to analyze these sentences into their grammatical constituents, but rather to see in a more general sense how they are built and when they are used.

Classroom Activity: Sentence Spotlight

Jeff Anderson has long been a proponent of calling attention to specific sentences in prose that the entire class has read. In *Everyday Editing* he states, "I got into a regular habit of spending time reading great sentences and talking about them. And a funny thing happened. The types of sentences we looked at and talked about started affecting their writing" (11). Here is my take on his approach:

- Point out a sentence that you think is interesting.
- Ask students a series of questions to elicit an analysis of its role in the passage and its general structure:
  1. What makes this sentence interesting or effective?
  2. What would change if we moved this over here? Or deleted this part?
  3. Which way do you prefer? Why?
  4. In what other ways could the author have expressed the same idea(s)?
  5. Why do you think the author decided to do it this way?
  6. Can you find other sentences that have one or more similar characteristics (punctuation, parallelism, grammatical structure, and so on)?
- After you have finished analyzing the sentence, have students change the topic and, using different words, write a sentence that is modeled after the target sentence.
- Encourage students to incorporate spotlighted sentences in their writing:
  1. For lower grades, put these spotlighted sentences on your classroom walls so that students can look around for inspiration as they are writing.
  2. For higher grades, ask students to keep a writer's log section in which they will accumulate the spotlighted sentences. They can review these sentences before or during the writing process.
- Note that, after students become familiar with this activity, you can substitute alternative selection processes for the spotlighted sentence:
  1. **Student-selected.** After they have read an assigned passage, ask students to go back and decide what sentence they thought was the most interesting. If the same sentence is chosen by more than one student, put it under the spotlight; otherwise, use the one that you, the teacher, have selected. This option encourages students to be more aware of sentence structure, either as they read or as they go back through the selection looking for a good spotlight candidate.
  2. **Essay-based.** Inform your class that you will select one or more sentences for a spotlight activity from the essays they hand in. This option encourages students to be more creative with their sentences, heightening sentence awareness in the process.

Classroom Activity: Name That Sentence

In her excellent book *Crafting Writers, K–6*, Elizabeth Hale extols the virtues of helping students to discover writers' craft in authentic literature. She helps students spotlight specific sentences, adding some interesting—and effective—layers to the process.

In the steps that follow, I will model how I do this in my classes, using a paragraph from a fourth-grade reading selection by Seymour Simon. (As before, I'm using a fourth-grade reading selection to show that these techniques are applicable from the upper elementary grades on up. Any level of reading material works beautifully for this activity.)

> Gray whales are huge animals. They reach a length of forty-five feet, as long as a bus, and a weight of thirty tons, as heavy as ten elephants. They spend most of their time below the water, surfacing every few minutes to take a breath and then disappearing into the depths again. Gray whales feed along the ocean bottom, blowing water out of their mouths, stirring up the sediment, and then sucking up the cloudy water with any living things that happen to be in it. The whale surfaces every few minutes to rinse its mouth and swallow the catch.

Step 1: Select a sentence. Find a sentence that is interesting to you. Here is my target sentence:

> Gray whales feed along the ocean bottom, blowing water out of their mouths, stirring up the sediment, and then sucking up the cloudy water with any living things that happen to be in it.

Step 2: Prepare questions. Jot down some questions to help students explore the target sentence. I use the first two questions all the time, followed by several "What if" questions. As Hale notes, "One way to figure out the Why behind craft techniques is to compare each one to a more basic choice an author . . . could have made. Thinking through other ways the text could have been written is an important aspect to seeing and understanding the craft of writing" (25).

1. What is interesting about this sentence? Why did I pick it to explore?
2. What makes it work? Why is it good?
3. What if I made this sentence into four sentences? Which version sounds better, and why?

Gray whales feed along the ocean bottom. They blow water out of their mouths. The water stirs up the sediment. Then they suck up the cloudy water with any living things that happen to be in it.

4. What if I put the series first? Better or worse?

    Blowing water out of their mouths, stirring up the sediment, and then sucking up the cloudy water with any living things that happen to be in it, gray whales feed along the ocean bottom.

5. The target sentence has three commas. Why is each one there? What if the writer failed to include them?

6. The first sentence of this paragraph begins with "Gray whales." The next two sentences begin with "They." Why do you think that the author decided to use "Gray whales" again to begin our target sentence instead of "They"?

Step 3: Name that sentence. Come up with a name for the technique embodied in the target sentence. I'm going to call this an Exploding Sequence sentence. Ask the class for naming suggestions before you show them yours. Have the class help you pick one.

Step 4: Create a template. Construct a template that captures the essence of the interesting aspect(s) of the target sentence. Here is a possible template for this sentence:

_____(General description of a process)_____, ___(-*ing* step 1) ___, ___(-*ing* step 2) ___, ___("and then" + -*ing* step 3) ___.

Step 5: Write another. Changing the topic and the words, write another sentence that imitates the original sentence. Here is my example for our target sentence:

We humans begin the digestion process by breaking food into smaller pieces, mixing in saliva, and then passing the food on to our esophagus for swallowing.

It has been my experience that some students will not be able to write an imitating sentence without the template. For whatever reason, they don't "see" the features of the targeted sentence that are so obvious to you. However, after some exposure to this type of activity, your students will be able to create their own templates and eventually skip the template step altogether, a sign of true progress!

As soon as possible after you have finished modeling the process, go through it again, but this time place more of the burden on the class.

- Ask the class to find an interesting sentence in a reading selection. (The second sentence of the whales paragraph would be my pick from this selection. See Table 5.1 for some of the details.)

- Ask if anyone wants to volunteer to be the teacher and lead the discussion, with your assistance, of course. (If nobody volunteers, then continue to lead the class.)

- Give your volunteer teacher help in formulating questions. Otherwise, he or she should be able to lead the class as they all work together to complete the remaining steps:

Name that sentence.

Create a template.

Write a similar sentence.

Once the students are familiar with Name That Sentence, ask them as part of their homework to find an interesting sentence, name it, create a template, and imitate it. Compare the results in class.

Finally, Hale suggests keeping a table of the sentences that are examined in this manner. For elementary students, keep a running table on a classroom wall for students to refer to while writing. For more advanced students, have them maintain the table in their writer's log. Table 5.1 provides two examples from our modeling activities—one we covered in detail, and one we simply alluded to.

TABLE 5.1. Name That Sentence

Name	Example	Remarks
Exploding Sequence	Gray whales feed along the ocean bottom, blowing water out of their mouths, stirring up the sediment, and then sucking up the cloudy water with any living things that happen to be in it.	Use –*ing* (participles) to show the steps of a process.
Length and Height	They reach a length of forty-five feet, as long as a bus, and a weight of thirty tons, as heavy as ten elephants.	Use similes to add details.

Sentences as Building Blocks

Creating perfectly crafted, nicely varied sentences will not, by itself, ensure that a passage is well written. In order to meet readers' expectations as they employ the sample-predict-confirm cycle, and in order to allow readers to interact successfully with a text, the sentences must be linked to each other, either by clearly visible or readily inferred connections. As Martha Kolln notes, "The first sentence in a paragraph, like the first paragraph of a chapter or essay, sets up expectations in the reader about what is coming. Certainly one of those expectations is that the following sentences will stick to the topic" (29–30).

Even though these linkages can be established in a wide variety of ways, four primary methods are most often employed to interrelate sentences. In each of these methods, a different way to establish a related topic in a new sentence is used. The topic comes from the previous sentence. Helping more advanced students see these four methods will provide a more tangible way for them to spot and repair GUESS errors; in addition, it will help them to see where further development is needed. The following demonstrations and activities will guide students as they figure out these four linking techniques.

Classroom Demonstration: Known-New Contract

Before you begin this demonstration, decide on a first name that is not a part of anyone's name in your class. I'll use George as my example. In class, as casually and naturally as possible in the normal flow of a conversation, ask this question: "Does anybody know George's last name?" Class members will surely try to figure out what you are talking about. You will normally get one of two responses:

1. More often than not, somebody in the class will say, "George who?" Depending on your reaction, this should elicit a chuckle or two. Point out that this response is perfectly natural, even though it makes no logical sense.

2. If nobody responds in this manner, they will probably ask questions such as "What 'George' are you talking about?" or "Who do you mean?"

Either of these two responses serves as a perfect introduction to your subject: the *known-new contract* (also called the *given-new contract*). Good writers don't throw new information at their readers arbitrarily. They communicate thoughts by constantly building from information that has already been established. In other words, *new* information is usually attached to *known* information. Another way to look at it is that most sentences consist of *topics* and *comments*. The *topic* of a given sentence should be *known* between writer and reader; the *comment* is *new* information—the raison d'être of the sentence.

All writers (and speakers) operate with this unspoken agreement in place. Violating it will make participants try to put things back in order—to reinstate this tacit contract. Let's apply this contract to my George example: for my question to make sense, the class should already have been talking about a specific George (the topic) prior to my question, making the targeted individual *known* information between us. I could then attach my request for *new* information (the comment, or, in this case, the question), thereby honoring the known-new contract. Once students understand this aspect of communication, they are ready to analyze writing to see how good writers incorporate it.

Classroom Activity: Topic-Comment Connections

Let me say up front that *topic-comment* relationships do not always lend themselves to neat and tidy categorizations and analyses. In a process essay, for example, step after step (comments or new information) may be given without actually tying each one back to the process (the topic or known information) being described. Why? Because the reader can easily infer the connections. However, the topic for a new sentence is usually generated from a nearby previous sentence by one of four methods. Helping student writers to discover these methods will give you, the writing teacher, some concrete concepts to employ as you work with your students to improve their writing.

In this activity, I will give an example of each of the four methods that writers most often use to interrelate sentences, using excerpts from Jonathan Kozol's "The Human Cost of an Illiterate Society" as examples. Help the class figure out the origin of topics for sentences subsequent to the first one in each excerpt, and assign each pattern a name. A series of questions and a brief discussion of the pattern follows each example.

Example 1

Illiterates cannot read the letters that their children bring home from their teachers. They cannot study school department circulars that tell them of the courses that their children must be taking if they hope to pass the SAT exams. They cannot help with homework. They cannot write a letter to the teacher. They are afraid to visit in the classroom. They do not want to humiliate their child or themselves.

1. In this example, pieces of new information (comments) are attached to the known topic of "illiterates," which is established in the first sentence. What did the writer do to let the reader know that every sentence after the first one is talking about the same topic—illiterates?

2. What name could you give this method?

David Brown describes this technique very succinctly: "[T]he writer simply repeats (directly or using some form of substitution) some or all of a previous topic" (86). In this example, Kozol does not repeat the topic (illiterates) over and over; instead, he opts to use a form of substitution—a pronoun. A simple name for this method is *topic repetition*.

Example 2

The U.S. military pays a high price too. Thirty percent of naval recruits were recently termed "a danger to themselves and to costly naval equipment" because of inability to read and understand instructions.

3. The first sentence establishes the topic ("the U.S. military") for this second example. But the second sentence does not repeat the topic. How does the second sentence develop its topic from the previous sentence?

4. What name could you give this method?

Rather than repeat the topic in the second sentence, the author provides an example that is *derived* from it. In this example, Kozol uses a general term at first ("military") and then a more specific term ("naval") to tie in the next sentence. Let's call this method *topic derivation*.

Example 3

One reason for the nation's incredulity, of course, is the deceptive impact of the U.S. census figures. Until recent years, these figures have been taken as authoritative indices of national reality.

5. The topic for the first sentence ("reason for the nation's incredulity") is not involved in the topic of the second sentence. Where does the new topic come from?

6. What name could you give this method?

In this example, the topic of the second sentence comes from the *comment* of the previous sentence: a word in the previous comment is repeated, either directly or by substitution, as the new topic. So we will call this method *comment repetition*.

Example 4

Many illiterates cannot read the admonition on a pack of cigarettes. Neither the Surgeon General's warning nor its reproduction on the package can alert them to the risks.

7. How does the second sentence obtain its topic from the first one?

8. What name could you give this method?

The topic of the second sentence does not involve repetition. Instead, it is derived, not from the topic of the previous sentence, but from the comment. This method is *comment derivation*.

To summarize, linkages between sentences are most often established by repetition or derivation.

1. **Topic repetition.** The topic established in an earlier sentence is repeated, directly or by substitution.

2. **Topic derivation.** A topic for a new sentence is derived from an already established topic.

3. **Comment repetition.** A word or phrase in the previous comment is repeated, directly or by substitution, in the topic of a following sentence.

4. **Comment derivation.** A topic for a new sentence is derived from the comment of a previous sentence.

These standard ways to link sentences are shown in Table 5.2.

TABLE 5.2. Sentence Linkage Summary

Technique	Graphic Representation	Example
1. Topic repetition	[Topic] + [comment] [Repeated topic] + [new comment]	Illiterates cannot read the letters.... They cannot study....
2. Topic derivation	[Topic] + [comment] [Derived from topic] + [new comment]	The U.S. military pays a high price too. Thirty percent of naval recruits ...
3. Comment repetition	[Topic] + [comment] [Repeated comment] + [New comment]	One reason for the nation's incredulity, of course, is the deceptive impact of the U.S. census figures. Until recent years, these figures ...
4. Comment Derivation	[Topic] + [comment] [Derived from comment] + [new comment]	Many illiterates cannot read the admonition on a pack of cigarettes. Neither the Surgeon General's warning nor its reproduction on the package ...

Classroom Application: Trace the Linkage—Professional Writing

Seeing how professional authors maintain the linkage between topic and comment from one sentence to the next is an excellent way to improve this skill in student writers. Following is the first paragraph of Annie Dillard's essay titled "Heaven and Earth in Jest." Let's see how she establishes these patterns to tie things together for her readers.

[1] A couple of summers ago I was walking along the edge of the island to see what I could see in the water, and mainly to scare frogs. [2] Frogs have an inelegant way of taking off from invisible positions on the bank just ahead of your feet, in dire panic, emitting a froggy "Yike!" and splashing into the water. [3] Incredibly, this amused me, and, incredibly, it amuses me still. [4] As I walked along the grassy edge of the island, I got better and better at seeing frogs both in and out of the water. [5] I learned to recognize, slowing down, the difference in texture of the light reflected from mudbank, water, grass, or frog. [6] Frogs were flying all around me. [7] At the end of the island I noticed a small green frog. [8] He was exactly half in and half out of the water, looking like a schematic diagram of an amphibian, and he didn't jump. (169)

I use a Sentence Linkage Worksheet for this type of analysis. Table 5.3 shows a completed one for the Dillard excerpt. A blank Sentence Linkage Worksheet is provided in Appendix C.

TABLE 5.3. Sentence Linkage Worksheet

Sentence Number	Source	Word or Phrase	#	New Topic	Method
1	☐ Topic √ Comment	frogs	2	frogs	√ Repeated ☐ Derived
2	☐ Topic √ Comment	an inelegant way of taking off …	3	this (substitution)	√ Repeated ☐ Derived
3	☐ Topic √ Comment	me	4	I	√ Repeated ☐ Derived
4	√ Topic ☐ Comment	I	5	I	√ Repeated ☐ Derived
5	☐ Topic √ Comment	frogs	6	frogs	√ Repeated ☐ Derived
6	☐ Topic √ Comment	me	7	I	√ Repeated ☐ Derived

Classroom Application: Trace the Linkage—Student Writing

Telling students that areas of their writing are not coherent doesn't help them very much. Showing them where things break down is a bit better. Letting *them* figure it out by tracing the linkages (or lack thereof) is easily the most effective thing a teacher can do. Three specific writing problems are especially germane here.

1. **GUESS error.** The most obvious problem is the GUESS error, which is often caused by poor or nonexistent linkages between sentences.

2. **Transition.** A second area, which overlaps the GUESS error problem, is the need for a transitional word, phrase, sentence, or even paragraph.

3. **Undeveloped information.** Brown notes, "Indeed, very often when teachers respond to a place in a student's essay with 'needs development,' the student has introduced some important new information but has failed to take it up in any subsequent sentence" (87).

The following four-sentence paragraph from a student's persuasive paper serves as a good example of the power of using linkages to address problems. The student was arguing in favor of allowing women to serve in combat duty. Here is her paragraph, exactly as I received it. As you read it, imagine how you might respond to it as her writing teacher.

> [1] In today's society and era war is inevitable. [2] Whether women should be in combat or not is being questioned. [3] U.S. Secretary of Defense Donald Rumsfeld stated, "It's an asymmetrical battlefield so there are not clear lines where battles are taking place on one side, and not the other." [4] The Combat Exclusion Act is a law and policy that restricts women from participating in positions that would require them to be in direct combat rather than serving in combat supporting roles.

I invited this student to step inside the mind of her reader: I asked her to fill out a Sentence Linkage Worksheet on this paragraph. Try it yourself before continuing to read.

One might be able to say that "war" and "combat" link the first two sentences, but the connection is weak at best. The first sentence introduces the new comment of inevitability, causing readers to GUESS that the next sentence, if not the entire paragraph, is about the inescapability of war. However, sentence 2 does not continue the "inevitability" discussion, but instead introduces a totally new topic. This new topic seems, once again, to be dropped in sentence 3: Rumsfeld's quote is totally disconnected from it. The Combat Exclusion Act information is likewise disconnected from sentence 3. Instead, it ties back to sentence 2, which is too far back for readers to handle. Readers can't infer clear connections, or draw on schemas or scripts to establish them. Because readers can't sample-predict-confirm with this paragraph, they are dead in the water.

How might a teacher respond to this paragraph in the absence of the linkage approach? One could say that sentence 1 needs development, that 2 needs a transition, and that 3 and 4 are GUESS errors. Or one might write a lengthy note explaining how this passage doesn't hang together, how it's not cohesive or coherent. Having students look for linkages, however, forces the writer to see things from her readers' perspective. Armed with this information, my student was able to make substantive revisions, thereby presenting her thoughts in a much more cohesive manner. Her rewrite also allowed me, as her reader, to see that the Rumsfeld quote fit in: today's counterinsurgent warfare is being fought not on battlefields, but in streets and houses of established neighborhoods. So excluding women from combat was tantamount to excluding them from military service in certain parts of the world. Readers certainly could not figure that out from her earlier version!

Summary

In this chapter we explored the concept of sentences from three perspectives.

- **Sentence definition.** The concept of *sentence* is extraordinarily difficult to pin down. We experimented with a few pseudo-definitions, and showed via demonstrations that none of them work. Despite the fact that we were unsuccessful at defining *sentence*, we showed via classroom activity that all of your students already have, albeit subconsciously, a pretty good feel for the concept and can readily create sentences.

- **Sentence gathering.** Most students have well-developed *receptive* skills with sentences: they can read and understand sentences that are often much more complex than the sentences they write (*productive* skills). An effective way to help students begin to incorporate more sophisticated sentence structures and techniques into their writing is to help them mine things they read for interesting sentences that embody strategies and structures that student writers could, with your help and encouragement, begin to incorporate into their own writing.

- **Sentence linkages.** For readers to be able to sample-predict-confirm and interact successfully with a piece of writing, sentences need to be linked to each other in some cohesive manner. We explored four primary ways that these linkages are maintained, using the concept of the known-new contract (or topic-comment). We also explored how to use this concept to help students see areas of their writing that need revision—further development, transitions, rearrangement, and so on.

Further Reading

For a more in-depth analysis of topic-comment, including some lesson plans for working with it, see David Brown's *In Other Words*.

For more information on mining sentences, see Jeff Anderson's *Everyday Editing* and Elizabeth Hale's *Crafting Writers, K–6* (don't let the title of this book fool you: you'll find useful suggestions, exercises, and activities for students at all grade levels.)

6

Exploring the Concept of Paragraph

By the time students come into our classroom, they have been exposed to thousands and thousands of professionally written paragraphs. They have also written dozens, if not hundreds, of paragraphs themselves. As a result, they have already accumulated quite a bit of knowledge, much of it, perhaps, unconscious, about what a paragraph should be. This chapter begins with a multi-step classroom activity that taps into that subconscious body of knowledge and raises it to a conscious level to build a definition of a paragraph (much as we did with sentences in Chapter 5)—a classic triple-X approach (as detailed in Chapters 4 and 5). Once a working definition is established (and this time, we *will* establish one), we explore what makes a paragraph hang together, revisiting sentence linkages in the process.

As we saw in Chapters 4 and 5, professionally written passages can be mined for writers' craft at the sentence level. The same is true at the paragraph level. We will also explore ways to help students see the "hidden" techniques and strategies that professional writers use to create interesting, varied, and cohesive paragraphs that deliver information efficiently.

Finally, we will address the phenomenon of paragraphs that do not stay on topic. If a writer suddenly changes directions in a paragraph, then a GUESS error occurs; however, if the change is gradual, then it becomes difficult to pin down exactly where the shift occurs. The only thing that readers know is that they came into a paragraph with one topic and ended on another related, but different topic.

Paragraph Definition

Rather than try to explain the qualities that make a paragraph work, why not let the students figure it out for themselves? The following four-step activity does just that, beginning with a very poor definition of a paragraph and working from there.

Classroom Activity: An Inadequate Definition of *Paragraph*

The following definition of a paragraph needs some serious work:

Definition 1. A paragraph is a group of sentences that are *separated* from other groups of sentences by indenting the first line and/or by skipping a line.

Read Paragraph Version A and answer the questions that follow.

Paragraph Version A

Hurricanes have been happening with greater frequency over the past few years. My sister drove into the back of another car yesterday. Soccer will probably never be as popular in the United States as it is in the rest of the world. As the price of gasoline increases, more people are buying smaller cars.

1. *According to definition 1*, is Version A a paragraph?

2. According to what you already know about paragraphs, is Version A a well-formed paragraph? Why or why not?

3. What is missing from definition 1?

A paragraph is certainly a unit of text that is marked visually by indentation and/or by spaces before and after it. Although it's important that the sentences form a visual unit, it is even more important that they form a *conceptual* unit. *A paragraph must deal with a single topic.* The above "paragraph" is about as bad as it can get: it deals with four absolutely unrelated topics. We obviously need to modify the definition.

The second definition improves on the previous one:

Definition 2. A paragraph is a group of sentences that deal with a *single topic*. These sentences are *separated* from other groups of sentences by indenting the first line and/or by skipping a line.

Read Paragraph Version B and answer the questions that follow.

Paragraph Version B

Cockroaches are not used to living on a polished floor. In the wild, most cockroaches do not die on their backs. The cockroaches that we see have often died from insecticide. Muscle spasms cause them to flip over on their backs. In nature, when they wind up on their backs, there is usually something for them to grab with their legs to right themselves. Insecticides destroy the nervous system of cockroaches. Most cockroaches die because they are eaten by other animals. Cockroaches always appear to die on their backs.[1]

1. *According to definition 2,* is Version B a paragraph?

2. According to what you already know about paragraphs, is Version B a well-formed paragraph? Why or why not?

3. What is missing from definition 2?

All of the sentences in Version B deal with a single topic: cockroaches dying on their backs. But the paragraph still doesn't make sense. Clearly, it isn't enough for the sentences to all relate to the same topic. They must also be arranged in some logical order. Again, we need to modify our definition.

The third definition improves on the previous one:

Definition 3. A paragraph is a group of *logically ordered* sentences that deal with a *single topic.* These sentences are *separated* from other groups of sentences by indenting the first line and / or by skipping a line.

Obviously, we need to rewrite Version B so that the thoughts are in logical order. Will that make it into a good paragraph?

Paragraph Version C

[1] Cockroaches always appear to die on their backs. [2] In the wild, most cockroaches do not die on their backs. [3] Most cockroaches die because they are eaten by other animals. [4] Cockroaches are not used to living on a polished floor. [5] In nature, when they wind up on their backs, there is usually something for them to grab with their legs to right themselves. [6] The cockroaches that we see have often died from insecticide. [7] Insecticides destroy the nervous system of cockroaches. [8] Muscle spasms cause them to flip over on their backs.

1. *According to definition 3,* is Version C a paragraph?

2. According to what you already know about paragraphs, is Version C a well-written paragraph? Why or why not?

3. What is missing from definition 3?

In a well-written paragraph, information is connected so that the reader can see how pieces of information relate to each other. In Version C, the sentences are in logical order, but, rather than being connected, they are strung together like beads on a necklace.

The definition needs one more piece of information to be complete:

> **Definition 4.** A paragraph is a group of *interconnected, logically ordered* sentences that deal with a *single topic*. These sentences are *separated* from other groups of sentences by indenting the first line and/or by skipping a line.

Version D, which follows, is a rewrite of this paragraph that interconnects the sentences into a cohesive passage. After you read it, we will look at a series of questions to help you contrast Version D with Version C in order to find out what the author did to Version C to link thoughts together so that you, the reader, could sample-predict-confirm much more easily.

Paragraph Version C

[1] Cockroaches always appear to die on their backs. [2] In the wild, most cockroaches do not die on their backs. [3] Most cockroaches die because they are eaten by other animals. [4] Cockroaches are not used to living on a polished floor. [5] In nature, when they wind up on their backs, there is usually something for them to grab with their legs to right themselves. [6] The cockroaches that we see have often died from insecticide. [7] Insecticides destroy the nervous system of cockroaches. [8] Muscle spasms cause them to flip over on their backs.

Paragraph Version D

[1] Cockroaches always appear to die on their backs. [2] However, in the wild, most cockroaches do not die on their backs; they die because they are eaten by other animals. [3] Indoors, two other factors come into play. [4] For one thing, cockroaches are not used to living on a polished floor. [5] In nature, when they wind up on their backs, there is usually something for them to grab with their legs to right themselves. [6] Another factor is that the dead cockroaches that we see often have died from an insecticide that destroys their nervous systems. [7] As a result, muscle spasms cause them to flip over on their backs.

Following are questions for discussion. (Answers appear in italics after each question.)

1. A word was added after sentence 1 in Version D. What is that word, and why was it added? *The word "However" allows readers to GUESS that the next sentence contrasts with the first.*

2. Version C sentences 2 and 3 are joined together as sentence 2 in Version D. How are they joined together and why? *They are joined by a semicolon to signal to readers that the two sentences are closely related.*

3. In Version D, a new sentence (sentence 3) is added. Why? *This new sentence is a transition. It allows readers to predict what comes next and ensures that they understand how this new information is related to the previous information.*

4. Sentence 4 of Version D has a new transition phrase: "For one thing." Why do you think the author put that phrase there? *To let readers know that the first of the "two other factors" is being addressed.*

4. Sentence 6 of Version D has a new transition phrase. What is it, and what purpose does it serve? *The transition ("Another factor") lets readers know that the second of the "two other factors" is being addressed.*

5. Version C sentences 6 and 7 are joined together as sentence 6 in Version D. Why did the author decide to join them? *The two sentences are repetitive and somewhat choppy. The joined sentence sounds more sophisticated.*

6. A transition phrase is added to sentence 7 in Version D. What is that phrase, and what kind of relationship does it indicate to the reader? *The phrase "As a result" shows that the information in the next sentence has a cause-and-effect relationship with the previous one: the insecticide causes the muscle spasms.*

We have seen four basic requirements for a properly constructed paragraph. The first item—separating paragraphs from each other—is a necessary, but simple requirement that needs no extra practice. The other three requirements—which deal with the *structure* of a paragraph—need some gentle, carefully constructed guidance.

Playing with Paragraphs

As we have already established, GUESS errors are not minor problem areas. Not only do they confuse readers, but they also reflect badly on the writer. We have spent a fair amount of time looking at GUESS errors at the sentence level;

however, equally egregious GUESS errors can be created when paragraphs do not relate closely to each other. Although it's true that a new paragraph is a signaling device for a change in topics, the new topic must be tied in to the fabric of what precedes it. Failure to do so is a common source of GUESS errors in student writing.

Classroom Activity: Multi-Paragraph Topic Maintenance

Select several paragraphs from a professionally written source, either literary or expository, that the students have not read. As a class, analyze the paragraphs to see how the author linked them.

- Show one paragraph to the class, asking the students to follow along as you read it aloud. Then ask the class to predict the general content of the next paragraph by asking students to respond to the following questions.

  1. GUESS what the next paragraph is about. (List the answers if more than one is suggested.)

  2. Show me the text that supports your GUESS.

  3. If your GUESS is correct, should the author use a transition in the next paragraph to help readers process the text smoothly? Why or why not?

  4. If a transition is advisable, what might be a good one?

- Reveal and read the next paragraph.

- Discuss the accuracy of GUESSes from the previous paragraph and the presence or absence of a transition in the new one.

- GUESS the next paragraph, using the discussion points just listed, and repeat this process for each paragraph.

The following is a sample from a topic maintenance exercise that I have used with my students. After each paragraph, I include a brief summary of the general content of my students' reactions. The text is taken from *The Tornado* by Thomas Grazulis.

Paragraph 1

The mystery of how and why tornadoes form, or tornadogenesis, may be decades away from a satisfactory explanation. Progress is very slow. From the time a hook echo was detected on conventional radar in 1953, it was fifteen years until a mesocyclone was detected on Doppler radar and then another twenty-seven years until a portable Doppler radar was able to get close enough to a tornado to reveal the complex airflow in and around an actual funnel. Here is a brief summary of these two events. (50)

Now, GUESS the next paragraph.

- **GUESS.** Only one GUESS is feasible here: the author must write about one of the "two events" that he refers to. To be more specific, he should discuss the events in the same order that he introduces them in the preceding paragraph.
- **Text in support.** The last sentence of this paragraph is a clear signal to readers about the direction and content of the next paragraph.
- **Transition?** No transition is necessary—the last sentence serves as a nice introductory transition for the next paragraph.

Paragraph 2

On August 9, 1968, 100-mph winds seemed to come out of nowhere at Marblehead, Massachusetts. Harbormaster John Wolfgram was unaware of rotating clouds overhead or that this storm was to become a part of meteorological history. His only concern was that dozens of boats were being destroyed in this small section of the Massachusetts coast. It was of no consequence to the boat owners that 20 miles west, at Sudbury, Ralph Donaldson was heading a research team that was beaming a radar signal into the storm, 3 miles over Wolfgram's head. (50)

And now GUESS the next paragraph

- **GUESS.** Two choices are possible:

  GUESS 1: a continuation of the discussion about the first event.

  GUESS 2: the beginning of the discussion about the second event.
- **Text in support.** Every class favors the first choice. Students feel certain that the author has piqued the curiosity of his readers with the following: "this storm was to become a part of meteorological history." So the author is obligated to explain why the beaming of the radar signal proved to be significant.
- **Transition?** If GUESS 1 is correct, then no specific transition is necessary. If GUESS 2 is correct, then students generally favor a transition.

- **Which transition?** If a transition is used, the most common suggestion is "The second event . . ." or "The other event . . ."

Paragraph 3

Donaldson was steering the radar beam horizontally, across the thunderstorm. The returning signal from a small area in the storm indicated motion toward the radar unit. Two miles to the right, motion was away from the unit. This meant that the storm was rotating. For the first time the rotation of a mesocyclone was detected by radar using the frequency shift in radiowaves known as the Doppler effect. The initial signs of rotation occurred one full hour before the storm hit Marblehead and ushered in an era in which we can study the rotary motions inside a potentially tornadic thunderstorm, even when the storm is up to 100 miles from the radar. (51)

GUESS the next paragraph.

- **GUESS.** The same two choices exist: continue the radar topic, or move on to the next event. But this time, the classes heavily favor moving on to the next event.

- **Text in support.** The last sentence in the paragraph sums up the importance of the event, so students infer that the writer will be moving on to the next event in the next paragraph.

- **Transition?** Most students feel that, if the author is moving on to the second event, some sort of transition would be nice just to make the change in topics crystal clear for readers.

- **Which transition?** Again, the most common suggestion is always "The second event . . ." or "The other event . . ."

The next paragraph does, indeed, move on to the second event, using the following signaling phrase to inform the readers of this change: "Twenty-seven years later . . ." We would continue to GUESS each paragraph in a similar manner.

We teach our students that a new paragraph signals a change in topics, yet we often fail to show them how paragraphs link together. And, of course, as we read, we pay scant attention to inter-paragraph connections unless the writer fails to maintain them. Helping students to verbalize inter-paragraph connections by tapping into their reading brains allows them to bring to the fore this often ignored facet of writing, thereby providing insight and ideas for their future writing tasks.

Classroom Application: Multi-Paragraph Topic Maintenance

Student problem areas. Analyzing well-connected paragraphs is an excellent way to build skills; seeing the contrast between successful linkages and poor or nonexistent ones provides excellent reinforcement. Start maintaining a collection of student GUESS errors caused by poor or nonexistent linkages between paragraphs (anonymously, of course). Once you begin collecting these, they accumulate pretty quickly. Show some to your classes so that you can discuss what went awry. Here is one from a former student that contains both a sentence- and paragraph-level GUESS error:

> She [my mother] was staring out at the deep blue sky. She always does this when she starts to think about my grandfather. He loved the snow and now that's all she has to remember him by. **[GUESS]**
> I loved to watch her do her hair. I'd try to imagine what she is thinking about, but today was different. **[GUESS next paragraph]**
>> Later, I found my way into the attic. My grandfather used to take me up there when I was little …

The second paragraph continues describing what the author and her grandfather found of interest in the attic; the essay never returns to her mother doing her hair. The context that the student's brain created as she was writing this is absolutely inaccessible to her readers.

Peer editing. This activity is perfect for peer-review sessions: students don't have to be strong writers to be able to make GUESSes. Pair your students and have them take turns GUESSing, one paragraph at a time, what comes next in each other's essays and then explaining why they think so. Seeing peers struggle with something students have written is usually much more effective than anything you, their teacher, could do or say.

On a related issue *(this is my transition phrase alerting you, my reader, that I am changing topics, but not to one that could be easily inferred from the previous paragraph)*, I have worked with many students who have been told that *every paragraph* must end with a sentence that serves as a lead-in to the following paragraph. This type of advice flies in the face of the reality of existing professionally written prose. In reality, writers only occasionally put sentences at the end of one paragraph that serve as specific links to the next one. Trying to force such a sentence in an attempt to adhere to this "rule" is the source of many GUESS errors in student writing. Rather than implement this patently false rule, use the topic maintenance activities just presented to help students discover how authors actually tie paragraphs together. Then help students develop this skill.

Classroom Activity: Mining Paragraphs

In Chapter 5, we explored mining sentences for writers' craft. Paragraphs can also be mined for techniques and structures that students can emulate in their writing.

- Find a paragraph or short passage that contains an interesting technique or structure.
- Ask questions to help students figure out how it works.
- Name the technique or structure.
- Supply students with ideas so that they can practice creating their own passages using this new method.

Let's walk through a sample paragraph that I have used in my classes (after having explored the concept of parallelism).

> It sometimes seems that everyone wants to improve schooling in America, but each in a different way. Some want to strengthen basic skills; others, critical thinking. Some want to promote citizenship or character; others want to warn against the dangers of drugs and violence. Some demand more from parents; others accent the role of community. Some emphasize core values; others, the need to respect diversity. All, however, recognize that schools play an essential role in preparing our children to become knowledgeable, responsible, caring adults. (Elias 1)

1. This paragraph contains one example of extended parallelism. Where does it begin and end? *It begins with the second sentence and ends with the next-to-last sentence.*

2. What is the structure of the extended parallelism? *"Some" + what is important to them + semicolon + "others" + what is important to them.*

3. Why did the author include the information that the extended parallelism contains? *To show wide differences of opinion about specific issues in education.*

4. What is the function of the last sentence? *To show one general area where everyone is in agreement about the importance of schools.*

5. What is the logical flow of this paragraph? *The author begins with a statement, followed by six examples (in parallel structure) to support his assertion. He ends with a general statement that applies to everyone.*

6. What could we name this kind of paragraph? *Parallel contrasts (or something like that).*

Your turn. Now, give students the chance to create their own paragraphs with these instructions:

- Put this paragraph away and write one that is similar in structure. You may create your own scenario or use the following:

    People enjoy sports, but for different reasons. Pick three to four of the following sports or substitute your own: football, basketball, baseball, soccer, tennis, boxing.

  End with a general statement that applies to everyone.

- If you don't like the sports example, develop any of the following subjects into a similarly structured paragraph:

    video games

    arts and crafts

    music

The previous example deals with structure—parallelism, to be specific. Here are some other areas that you can explore at the paragraph or short passage level:

- What transitions did the author use to tie things together?
- How did the author establish voice?
- How did the author express emotion?
- Did the author use variety in sentence length?
- Did the author use variety in structures—sentence beginners, interrupters, expanders? (See my book *Unleashing Your Language Wizards*.)
- Can you either create or revise a paragraph to look like this one?

Scope Creep

I borrowed the term *scope creep* from the business world. The website Business-Dictionary.com defines scope creep as "small changes in a plan or project that necessitate other changes which lead to still more changes . . . and so on." In the writing arena, I use the term to label a rather commonly occurring phenomenon: readers set up expectations for a paragraph based on the context that precedes it and/or by its topic sentence(s). These expectations become part of the sample-predict-confirm process, influencing predictions of general direction and content. Student writers can create a subtle type of GUESS error by violating these expectations in two ways. See if your students can derive the two ways from the following activity.

Classroom Activity: Two Types of Scope Creep

When a reader begins to read a new paragraph, the topic is quickly established. If the writer suddenly switches topics, that is, heads off in an unexpected direction, a GUESS error occurs. It is possible, however, for a writer to *gradually* change topics—to drift off target. No GUESS error occurs in this scenario because the shift is too gradual; yet, by the end of the paragraph, the reader is puzzled or surprised by the change in direction. In other words, a paragraph may be narrowly defined at the beginning, but the writer gradually moves off into other directions so that, by the time the reader finishes the paragraph, an understated type of GUESS error occurs: readers find themselves working with information that lies outside the realm of expectations that was created at the beginning of the paragraph.

The following two paragraphs, taken directly from student compositions, illustrate the two common ways in which writers move away from the topic they have established for that paragraph. Read each paragraph and try to name each of these methods.

Paragraph 1

Landscaping is also good for homeowners as it can help with utility bills. A large shade tree over a house can keep the house cooler in the summer and warmer in the winter. Well placed trees and hedges can also help block wind and snow. Doing landscaping can also make a house look more fun. Also, having landscaping can maximize the space of a yard, especially if it is a small yard. The more landscaping that is done, the less yard that needs to be mowed, which most people would see as a definite advantage. Having fountains, gazebos, and barbeque pits increases the property value because they double as entertainment areas.

Name the type of scope creep.

Paragraph 2

I will thank my parents for the rest of my life for their decision to home school me. Not only did I gain so much knowledge from home schooling, but I also learned so much about life: I learned how to communicate with the elderly, I learned how to be a grown up, and my father also instilled in me the love for music. He had such a passion for music. My love for music is a gift that my father left behind for me and I thank him every day for it.

Name the type of scope creep.

Paragraph 1. The first sentence of this paragraph leads the reader to believe that this paragraph is going to discuss how landscaping can save money on utility bills. The next two sentences reinforce that expectation. However, the scope of the paragraph is broader than that—it's not restricted to utility bills, as the first three sentences lead readers to assume. We might call this *expanding scope creep*.

The fix here is easy. Begin this paragraph in a manner that allows the reader to anticipate the broader scope. The writer could, for example, have begun the paragraph this way: "Landscaping has several advantages for homeowners." Now the reader is in a position to make good predictions that are easily confirmed by subsequent reading.

Paragraph 2. This student started off writing about the advantages of home schooling, but by the time we get to the end, she is writing about her gift of music—this is classic scope creep. There is no single place where you could mark the occurrence of a GUESS error; everything is connected to what precedes it. The problem, of course, is that the scope, the established topic, morphed into something else at the end. We might call this *drifting scope creep*.

The fix here requires some major surgery. This "paragraph" has two related, but distinct topics: the advantages of home schooling and the love for music that the writer's father gave her. The writer has three options:

1. Delete the music topic.
2. Relate the music topic to the home schooling advantages topic. For example, instead of writing "and my father also instilled in me the love for music," the writer could have started a new sentence with a transition that links the two topics: "Finally, if I hadn't been home schooled, my father would not have had the time he had to instill in me the love for music."
3. Start a new paragraph about her father and the love for music.

The concept of scope creep is very easy for students to grasp, especially if they understand the sample-predict-confirm concept. I use a crosshairs illustration to represent scope creep graphically. Figure 6.1 shows a blank example, and Figures 6.2 and 6.3 show the illustrations filled in to match each of our two sample paragraphs. Once students understand this phenomenon, all you have to do is label any paragraph that contains scope creep. Your students will have no trouble seeing scope creep in the paragraph you label. They may or may not need assistance in resolving the issue, but spotting it will be easy.

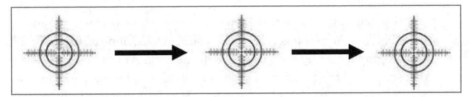

FIGURE 6.1. Blank scope creep graphic.

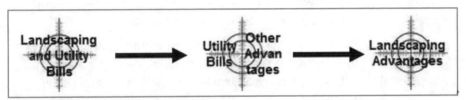

FIGURE 6.2. Scope creep graphic for paragraph 1.

FIGURE 6.3. Scope creep graphic for paragraph 2.

Summary

A primary consideration for student writers to keep in mind is *how are readers going to process my paragraph(s)*? Will they be aware of the linkages between sentences and paragraphs? Will they be able to sample-predict-confirm readily? Are they going to self-google relevant information? Are they going to make good inferences? How can I structure my paragraph(s) so that readers walk away with the message that I want to deliver?

In this chapter we explored the concept of paragraphs from these perspectives:

- **Paragraph definition.** Using an inquiry-based approach, we gradually built a definition of a paragraph using a trial-and-error method. The resulting definition: A paragraph is a group of *interconnected, logically ordered* sentences that deal with a *single topic*. These sentences are *separated* from other groups of sentences by indenting the first line and/or by skipping a line.

- **Multi-paragraph topic maintenance.** To explore how professional authors link paragraphs together, we had students examine texts paragraph by paragraph, asking them to GUESS the next paragraph, show the text that supported their GUESS, decide whether the author needed a transition into the next paragraph, and, if so, which transition might be used.

- **Paragraph mining.** In a manner similar to mining professionally written prose for good sentence devices and techniques, we saw how to examine a text for good paragraphing devices and techniques.

- **Scope creep.** If a writer makes a sudden shift within a paragraph, this change of direction results in a GUESS error. But if a writer makes a gradual transition, with no clear area to mark where the topic either expanded or changed, readers will be confused by the transition but unable to note specifically where it occurred. We called this type of gradual GUESS error scope creep, and we identified two types: expanding scope creep and drifting scope creep.

Note

1. I created this paragraph using information from "The Cockroach," http://www.bio.umass.edu/biology/kunkel/cockroach_faq.html#Q6.

Exploring the Concept of Essay

Chapters 5 and 6 explored fundamental building blocks of any piece of writing: sentences and paragraphs. In this chapter, we advance to the essay level. We begin by examining the four principle components of an essay: the title, introduction, body, and conclusion. We then move on to more holistic aspects of essays: voice and genre. In keeping with the previous chapters, all of these explorations will be from the triple-X approach (see Chapter 4), tapping into what students already know and building from there. We will end this chapter with a brief analysis of the research paper: how what we so often work on in classrooms matches teacher expectations, perhaps, but differs from the actuality of writing tasks that take place in the real world.

Essay Parts

As Stanley Fish so aptly notes, "Content just sprawls around; forms constrain and shape it" ("What Should Colleges Teach"). The essay is, of course, the primary form that we teach in the classroom. And as Lisa Donohue states, "Before students are asked to write a piece in a particular form, they need to develop their background knowledge about it. They need to have some exposure to the components and purpose associated with the form of writing" (11). In fact, students in the upper grades have already had considerable exposure to a substantial amount of well-constructed writing—perhaps not essays per se, but good, professional writing that consists of titles or subtitles, introductions, bodies, and conclusions. Because of this exposure, their reading brains subconsciously predict these divisions; process them at a level below awareness; and, if they are ever omitted, are uncomfortable in their absence. This is a rich body of triple-X knowledge upon which to build.

Title Plus Introduction

In Chapter 3 we looked at a demonstration dealing with a paragraph titled "The Prisoner" to show how a title compels the brain to google itself for background information relative to the words in the title or the concept(s) that the title invokes. This self-googling process influences how readers interact with and understand the remainder of the piece. I have yet to find a more powerful way to show students the effect of a title on readers. In the classroom activity that follows, we will expand our horizons by briefly exploring how the title can work in combination with the introduction to allow readers to make good GUESSes.

Classroom Activity: Missing Pieces

Tell your class to imagine that they are reading an article, and that this is the first paragraph:

> The professor had a remarkable collection. It reflected not only the needs of his vocation—he taught nineteenth- and twentieth-century literature—but a book lover's sensibility as well. The shelves were strictly arranged and the books themselves were in superb condition. When he left the room we set to work inspecting, counting, and estimating. This is always a delicate procedure, for the buyer is at once anxious to avoid insult to the seller and eager to get the goods for the best price. We adopted our usual strategy, working out a lower offer and a more generous fallback price. But there was no need to worry. The professor took our first offer without batting an eye. (Birkerts 89–90)

Following are questions for discussion. (Student answers appear in italics after each question.)

1. What is the main unanswered question that you would like to ask the author about this paragraph? *Why is the professor selling his books?*
2. Why do you think that the author would be able to answer your questions? *The author must have had that information in mind when he wrote the paragraph.*
3. What does the author need to do so that this article makes better sense to her readers? *Provide some background information about this book sale.*

Actually, the paragraph you just read is the second paragraph in the article. The first paragraph is as follows. Read it, and then reread the previous paragraph.

Some years ago, a friend and I comanaged a used and rare book shop in Ann Arbor, Michigan. We were often asked to appraise and purchase libraries—by retiring academics, widows, and disgruntled graduate students. One day we took a call from a professor of English at one of the community colleges outside Detroit. When he answered the buzzer I did a double take—he looked to be only a year or two older than we were. "I'm selling everything," he said, leading the way through a large apartment. As he opened the door of his study I felt a nudge from my partner. The room was wall-to-wall books and as neat as a chapel. (Birkerts 89)

4. How does this paragraph prepare readers for the second paragraph? For the rest of the article? *It provides some background—at least readers know how the buyers and the professor got together.*

5. Would readers who had not already read the second paragraph be able to make good GUESSes about its content? *Absolutely.*

6. Do readers know now why the professor is selling all of his books? *No.*

7. The title of the article is "Into the Electric Millennium." After reading this title, can you now infer why the professor is selling his books? *Yes—he is probably able to access most, if not all, of his books digitally.*

8. The main point of this article is not the purchasing of this professor's books. What would you GUESS is the main thrust of this article? *The article must be about the move from print to digital media.*

9. What role does the professor's book sale probably play in the essay? *The opening paragraphs probably serve as an example—one person who sees the handwriting on the wall and appreciates the advantages of digital books.*

This exercise allows students to experience how a title and an introduction can combine to set the table for readers, allowing them to tap into their background knowledge; bring information to the foreground; put some pieces together; and, as a result, make good GUESSes about the content and general direction of a piece of writing. In this example, the first paragraph establishes background information that allows readers to understand why the author is buying these books. Simultaneously, it introduces a question that the second paragraph does not answer: why the professor is selling them. Still, the title helps the reader make a good GUESS about this unanswered question: the professor is probably switching over to digital texts. Given this well-founded GUESS, the reader can already make three reasonable GUESSes about where this piece of writing is headed.

1. The essay might be about this professor's switch.

2. The professor's situation might serve as an example to introduce an analysis of the ever-increasing move from print to electronic versions.

3. The title and introductory text might set up a more general discussion of the wide-ranging transition to computerization across all aspects of society.

Writers must produce titles and introductory text that facilitates GUESSes such as these; proficient readers draw such inferences from well-structured texts and are much more efficient in processing the remaining text as a result.

The Introduction

In Chapter 3 we established the primary purpose of an introduction: to allow the reader to GUESS the general content, direction, and (optionally) structure of a piece of writing. A secondary purpose is to grab the reader's attention—a point that is often discussed in writing texts and one that I will not, therefore, deal with in any detail here.

Student writers typically have a difficult time creating effective introductions. Daniel Willingham hints at a primary contributor to this difficulty:

> [W]e find *successful* thinking pleasurable. We like solving problems, understanding new ideas, and so forth. Thus we will seek out opportunities to think, but we are selective in doing so; we choose problems that pose some challenge but that seem likely to be solvable, because these are the problems that lead to feelings of pleasure and satisfaction. (14)

From a student writer's perspective, crafting an introduction appears to be a problem that is *not* very solvable.

- Student writers, influenced by its physical position in an essay, often try to write the introduction first. Yet writers are often ill prepared to create an introduction before writing the body, a point to which I will return later in this chapter.

- Introductions, from a student's perspective, are too amorphous. We typically tell students to grab the reader's attention, provide background information, and then bring the reader down to the specific thesis of the essay; however, we too often fail to give them specific strategies or options to help them do so. It's somewhat like describing the purpose of swimming to student swimmers, throwing them into the deep end, and then wondering why they flounder or drown.

- Finally, we frequently fail to make clear the primary purpose of an introduction: to allow the reader to make good GUESSes about the content of the piece of writing.

Readers don't normally pay attention to the devices that a proficient writer uses to prepare them for the content that she wishes to impart. Some teacher assistance is required. Let's look at a three-step approach that will help student writers understand the craft of creating effective introductions.

Step 1: List some possible introductory devices. Students can use these in their introductions. Be sure to emphasize that writers often use more than one of these devices as they craft their openings:

1. Provide an intriguing example.
2. Tell an interesting brief story or anecdote that sets up or pertains to your topic.
3. Give pertinent statistics.
4. Ask a challenging question or questions.
5. Use a provocative quotation.
6. Make a useful analogy.
7. Define a term used throughout the essay.
8. Frame the body. Start one of the previous seven devices in the introduction, and then resolve it in the conclusion. One might, for example, ask a provocative question in the introduction and answer it in the conclusion. Or one might begin a relevant story and finish it in the conclusion. Used properly, framing is a very powerful tool.

Step 2: Identify the devices. In learning to write, as in many areas of learning, recognition should precede production. Give students examples of the various devices listed in part 1. Here are two ways:

1. Create your own set of introductions as detailed in Step 3, which follows. Then ask students to identify each introductory device (from Step 1) that you used.
2. As you read student essays and professional writing, look for good examples of introductory devices. You will very quickly build a collection

that encompasses all of the eight devices. Ask students to identify which device(s) the authors employed in your collection. Here are two examples from introductions that we looked at earlier:

- The "Good Introduction" that we examined in Chapter 3 employed device 6—an analogy of the stranger with your child—to set up a discussion of the effects of television ads on children.
- The introduction that we examined in the previous exercise (the professor selling all of his books) could be called device 1 or 2.

Keep revisiting these introductory devices. As you examine various common readings across the school year, be sure that one of your discussion points asks students to identify which device(s) authors used in their introductions.

Step 3: Use the devices. The next step involves creating introductions—artificially at first—that employ a variety of the devices. Begin by modeling the exercise: show your students a topic, and then give them examples of several introductions that, in aggregate, employ all eight devices, either singly or in combination. The students' job is to identify which device(s) you used in each instance. For example, if the topic is credit card dangers, show students different openings that use all eight of the devices.

Now it's their turn. Here is one way to get things started:

- Divide the class into eight groups—one for each introductory device.
- Have the groups draw numbers (1 through 8) to see what device each group should use.
- Provide the class with a single topic. (Persuasive writing topics work best.)
- Ask each group to write a complete introduction that employs the assigned device. I allow them to "invent" facts or figures for this exercise, reminding them that such inventions are forbidden in any other writing situation.
- Read and discuss the introductions, asking the class questions such as these:
  1. Which version do you prefer? Why?
  2. What are the strengths and weaknesses of each version?
  3. Which devices might be combined to strengthen the introduction?
  4. How are readers' GUESSes changed or influenced by each version?

Finally, as students write papers to be graded, ask them to identify the introductory device(s) that they have used by writing the number(s) that correspond to the device(s) in the margins.

The Conclusion

Have you ever watched a movie that, without warning, just ended? Caught by surprise, you are left with questions about what happened to characters or how situations were resolved. At the other end of the spectrum is the movie that creates such a strong feeling of closure at the end that the audience begins to get up and leave before the credits start to roll.

Occasionally, a creative writer will end a story by simply stopping, without resolving some or any of the conflicts it contains. This type of rhetorical device may be occasionally acceptable in the creative world, but not in the academic or business worlds. When readers reach the concluding paragraph(s), they should have a clear sense (GUESS) that the essay is coming to an end, and, when they read the last sentence, they should know that the essay is over. Too often, student writers just quit, leaving the readers looking on the back side of pages for the rest of the essay. A vital role of a conclusion, therefore, is to allow readers to GUESS that the essay is ending.

The Writing Center at the University of North Carolina at Chapel Hill offers the following summation of the role of a conclusion: "Just as your introduction acts as a bridge that transports your readers from their own lives into the 'place' of your analysis, your conclusion can provide a bridge to help your readers make the transition back to their daily lives. Such a conclusion will help them see why all your analysis and information should matter to them after they put the paper down" ("Conclusions").

Any of the eight devices that we examined for introductions (page 113) can also be used in conclusions, either singly or in combination. Add two more devices to this list:

Call for action or awareness.

Make observation(s) about the future.

For recognizing and, later, for using conclusion devices, follow the same steps you followed for introduction devices.

The Body

One of my perspectives in this book is to encourage you to expose your students to what goes on in readers' brains as they process text, and to show how that processing should affect the organization and structure of a piece of writing. From that perspective, two areas impact the creation of the body of an essay, one of which we have covered in considerable detail, and one to which we must devote more attention:

1. How the reader's brain functions in the presence of written text. This functioning includes the sample-predict-confirm cycles, the GUESS error, economy of effort (EofE), background information (self-googling), and inferring—concepts that we covered in the first three chapters of this book.

2. How the reader's brain craves both variety *and* consistency.

Variety. Is variety truly the spice of life? From the brain's perspective, it certainly is. The human brain is constantly being bombarded by data from within (temperature, breathing, pain sensors, heartbeat, and so on) and from without (aural, oral, tactile, linguistic, social, and so on). Although the brain can handle huge volumes of data, it cannot begin to deal with the truly staggering amount of incoming data that constantly assails it. Because the brain's primary function is to protect the organism, it downplays or ignores information that appears to pose no threat, while elevating potential dangers to higher levels of attention. Here are two examples of these pervasive phenomena:

* You are asleep deep in the jungle of Africa when suddenly you are awakened by—total silence. Inured to the normal noises of the night, your brain lights up at the uncommon stillness and elevates this oddity to a level that rouses you.

* You are at a cocktail party, chatting with a small group of people and ignoring the hum of conversations in other groups around you. However, when someone in a group near you happens to mention your name, you "hear" that and begin listening to what this other group is saying, tuning out the conversation of the group you are in. (This behavior has a name in the field of psycholinguistics: the cocktail party phenomenon.)

This facility of downplaying repetitious, but nonthreatening input makes perfect sense when dealing with day-to-day survival in the real world—another example of EofE—but it becomes an obstacle to overcome when working in the writing world. Readers become bored and lose focus when reading the same sentence structure over and over; when reading nothing but short, choppy sentences; or when reading nothing but long, involved sentences.

Chapter 4 deals with the issue of structural diversity. It provides ways to help students see how professional authors infuse variety into their writing. The ultimate goal of this exposure is to encourage students to incorporate professional techniques and strategies into their own writing. I will briefly touch upon two areas not covered in that chapter:

1. Word repetition. Using the same word repeatedly sounds silly. This point can be easily demonstrated by substituting the antecedent for every pronoun that is used in a passage. Imagine, for example, that Jack London had used "Buck" instead of pronouns in the following snippet:

   > The next Buck knew, Buck was dimly aware that Buck's tongue was hurting and that Buck was being jolted along in some kind of a conveyance. The hoarse shriek of a locomotive whistling a crossing told Buck where Buck was.

   This is an extreme example of word repetition, but it demonstrates the effect nicely.

2. Sentence length. A passage of nothing but short sentences is childish and boring. A passage of nothing but long sentences is equally boring and, potentially, overwhelming. A mixture helps keep readers mentally alert. (For a more in-depth examination of sentence length, see my book *Unleashing Your Language Wizards*.)

Consistency. While variety is necessary in order to hold readers' attention, certain types of consistency are also necessary to create a cohesive, coherent piece of writing.

- Topics. Consistency of topic, within both paragraphs and essays, is absolutely required for the receptive brain to successfully reconstruct the tapestry of thoughts that the writer intends. GUESS errors and scope creep, introduced in Chapters 1 and 6 respectively, are excellent, tangible indicators that student writers have failed to maintain this critical type of consistency.

- Parallelism. Though structural variety on the whole helps to prevent readers from being lulled to sleep by repetitiveness, student writers need to understand that structural uniformity can, at times, be very helpful:

it allows readers to tie together series of thoughts and process them smoothly. Enter parallelism—the requirement that elements in a series maintain structural uniformity. This regularity enables readers to infer that items (words, phrases, clauses, or paragraphs) belong together, at the same level of importance, each building toward a unified whole. The net result is that parallelism creates a harmony that is pleasing to the reader's "ear" while also helping to create a positive impression of the writer.

- Voice. Student writers are too often plagued by an inability to create and maintain a consistent voice in a piece of writing. The good news is that, as students age, they gain increasing mastery over the ability to establish and maintain a voice—when speaking. However, as we have seen in so many aspects of their language, this mastery occurs, for the most part, at a level below consciousness. And thus we return to a basic maxim for teaching voice:

  > Students cannot learn to create and maintain a consistent voice until they learn to recognize it.

  Here are several activities that will help students begin to recognize voice in the writing of others and to see how authors fashion that voice with the relatively impoverished set of tools available to writers (in contrast to speakers).

  1. Voice identification. Select a passage from an assigned reading that exhibits a strong sense of voice. Prepare questions for students about the writer's voice: questions that examine the educational level, personality, geographical origin, emotion (angry, passionate, excited, nervous, persuasive, neutral, biased, factual, happy, fake, and so on), and age of the author. These questions can be open ended or multiple choice. Divide students into groups, and have each group answer the questions. Compare and contrast the responses.

  2. Voice analysis. Then ask the same groups to decide what features in the author's language convinced them to answer as they did. Try to come to a classroom consensus for each of the questions based on these features.

  3. Voice detection and imitation. Have students select passages that exhibit a strong sense of voice. These passages can come from anything your students are reading—from class assignments (yours or others) to

advertisements to emails to text messages (yes, even those have voice!). Ask each student to submit the following: a brief description of the context of the passage; a description of the voice that was created; an analysis of the language that created the strong voice; and a passage on an entirely different topic that creates a similar voice using the same language traits as the original passage.

4. Voice imagination. Pick two characters from something the class is reading. The greater the difference in voice between these two characters, the better. Ask students to write a letter, first as one character might have written it and next as the other one might have written it.

5. Voice application. Ask students to pick an event in their lives and write it as if they were writing it for their friends to read. (Warning: be sure to ask them, for classroom purposes, to keep the language clean even if they might not do so in reality.) Then ask students to write up the same event as if they were handing it in for a grade. Read some of the better pairs to the class (anonymously, of course), discussing what the writers did to establish voice in both versions.

A Blueprint for Writing

After determining the topic and general content of an essay, student writers typically want to write an essay in the same physical ordering as the various components that comprise it: the title, the introduction, the body, and then the conclusion. However, this certainly is *not* the most logical way to create an end result that will be interesting to readers. Students stand a much better chance of achieving this goal if they can work in an environment that more closely replicates the scenario that exists in real-world writing.

Ken Lindblom notes that in the real, noncreative writing sphere, "a composer addresses an audience to effect some purpose or form of action" (*English Journal* 99.6 14), something that is often called a rhetorical situation (see "The Rhetorical Situation" for details). But all too often, the classroom writing environment is more of a write-this-because-the-teacher-requires-it situation. When setting up a writing assignment, you should do your best to establish a rhetorical situation. Rather than just providing a prompt, set up an environment that allows you to specify who the potential audience is and what students are trying to accomplish with a piece of writing. Then ask students to employ the following blueprint as they work:

1. Establish the topic and the general content of the essay by research, brainstorming, reflection, and so on.

2. Draft the conclusion *before writing anything else*. (Require students to do this.) Stephen Covey wrote a best-selling business book titled *The Seven Habits of Highly Effective People*. Habit 2 advises to always *begin with the end in mind*. This maxim certainly pertains to writing. Beginning with the end in mind is a very good way to reinforce your established rhetorical situation and instill a real-world sense in a classroom setting. Of course, as the body of a piece of writing takes shape, the conclusion may need to be modified, but having an endpoint clearly established not only more closely replicates real-world scenarios, but also helps keep students focused as they compose the body.

3. Draft the body. Once student writers have a clearly established endpoint in mind, they can build toward it more effectively when planning the details and writing the body of their essays. Students should constantly be asking themselves whether a given segment helps move readers toward the stated target; without a clear objective in mind, their writing can more easily wander aimlessly.

4. Draft the introduction. Again, the single most important function of an introduction is to allow readers to GUESS the topic, general content, and direction of the piece of writing. How could anyone hope to set the stage properly for a play, the exact content of which has yet to be determined? Obviously, once student writers have written the body, they are in a much better position to craft introductions that prepare readers for that content.

5. Create a title. Writers can draft a title at any point in the writing process, but they need to be sure to review the title once everything else is successfully drafted.

6. Revise the text. So often, when student writers reread the products of their writing efforts, they do so by holding conversations with themselves: Do I understand this? Is this logical to me? Instead, during revision, writers should be holding "conversations" with potential readers: Will they understand what I am trying to convey? Will they be able to process the writing (that is, sample-predict-confirm) easily and accurately? Will they be upset or irritated by my language? Will they view me as someone who is competent?

The Research Paper Genre

Deborah Dean defines *genre* as "discourse that arises out of recurring communicative acts in certain social situations" (*Genre Theory* 54). She goes on to note that "students will imitate the genres they are familiar with. . . . students fall back on the models they know—for genre, for tone, for organization" (59). We need to ask ourselves these questions: What, exactly, do we mean by a research paper? What genre(s) are students exposed to while doing the research? How does the whole affair relate to the real-world demands and expectations of readers our students are likely to encounter?

Randy Bomer maintains that the traditional research paper is but one of six nonfiction categories (175). I divide his first category (to inform) into two: information and reporting. Table 7.1 shows an overview of the resulting seven nonfiction categories.

Bomer then makes the following observation: "The perceived demands of schools . . . have caused us to create and proliferate nongenres deeply entrenched in our assumptions about school writing, genres with no correspondence to the world outside school, genres no one ever chose to write" (170). He goes on to explain that when we assign a research paper and send students to the library or Internet to do research, they primarily consult sources that were written with

TABLE 7.1. Nonfiction Categories

Categories	Rhetorical Situation	Examples
Information	Writing to enlighten readers who seek knowledge about a specific subject	Encyclopedias, dictionaries, newspaper articles
Reporting	Writing to provide results and details of experimentation, research, or analysis	Science or business reports
Persuasion	Writing to convince readers to accept my position on a topic	Editorials, argumentation, advertisements
Expansion	Writing to demonstrate to readers that a given subject or individual is more complex and interesting than they had thought	Some magazine or newspaper articles, individual profiles
Exploration	Writing to try out an idea on readers	Essays, op-ed columns
Guidance	Writing to help readers who seek advice, assistance, or directions	Travel guides, book or movie reviews, self-help texts, manuals
History	Writing to tell readers the story behind certain events or people	Biographies or autobiographies, historical narratives

one rhetorical situation in mind: to inform readers who have come seeking the specific essentials it contains (the Information category in Table 7.1). Because that is the style to which students are exposed, that is the style that they emulate when they write. As a consequence, the rhetorical situation for which students are writing their research papers bears little resemblance to any rhetorical situation that most of them will encounter when they leave school. The resulting products are meaningless both to the student writers and to their potential readers (normally, just you, the teacher).

Jack Baker and Allen Brizee offer the following contrast between what research papers often are and what they should be: "A research paper is not simply an informed summary of a topic by means of primary and secondary sources. . . . The goal of a research paper is not to inform the reader what others have to say about a topic, but to draw on what others have to say about a topic and engage the sources in order to thoughtfully offer a unique perspective on the issue at hand."

It is, of course, very difficult to create a rhetorical situation in the classroom that will precisely replicate something your students may encounter later on. However, we can move away from the cut-and-paste format that the traditional research paper fosters to areas that are more appealing, more challenging, and less restrictive. The I-Search paper is one interesting example.

The I-Search Paper

The I-Search format requires each student to identify a question of *great personal interest*, to research that question, and to respond to it from a personal point of view. This objective is critical to the success of the writing venture. Wanting to answer a question that, somehow, pertains to them and their lives is a sizable step in the direction of creating a more authentic rhetorical situation.

The final product consists of three sections:

a. The story of your search: An explanation of what the writer knew about the subject before researching it, what he or she wanted to find out, and what steps were taken in order to find it out. This section much more closely resembles how true business reports, scientific write-ups or scholarly writings begin than the introductions required for most research paper assignments.

b. What you learned: Answers that you found as a result of your research and new questions that the research generated—issues that await further research.

c. Your reflections on the search: An analysis of what you learned about "conducting and documenting a search." ("Writing an I-Search Paper")

Googling "I-Search paper" will provide you with a wealth of information about this type of writing assignment.

Plagiarism

One area of the reading brain that I have found particularly useful in preventing plagiarism is the intuitive feel for style that students develop over the years as they work with a variety of reading materials. I spent years warning my students at the beginning of every semester not to yield to the temptation to try to pass off somebody else's writing as their own. I told them that I could spot plagiarism very easily, so they should not even attempt it. In vain. Every semester I would have at least one student who would plagiarize on a research report. Every semester, without fail. Then one day it dawned on me that *telling* students wasn't the answer—I had to *show* them by letting them use their own reading brains to spot plagiarism themselves.

Brenda Spatt has an exercise that embodies this approach. I follow her instructions, asking my students to find the plagiarized sentences in her paragraph:

> The Beatles' music in the early years was just plain melodic. It had a nice beat to it. The Beatles were simple lads, writing simple songs simply to play to screaming fans on one-night stands. There was no deep, inner meaning to the lyrics. Their songs included many words like I, and me, and you. As the years went by, the Beatles' music became more poetic. Sergeant Pepper is a stupefying collage of music, words, background noises, cryptic utterances, orchestral effects, hallucinogenic bells, farmyard sounds, dream sequences, social observations, and apocalyptic vision, all masterfully blended together on a four-track tape machine over nine agonizing and expensive months. Their music was beginning to be more philosophical, with a deep, inner, more secret meaning. After it was known that they took drugs, references to drugs were seen in many songs. The "help" in Ringo's "A Little Help from My Friends" was said to have meant pot. The songs were poetic, mystical: they emerged from a self-contained world of bizarre carnival colors; they spoke in a language and a musical idiom all their own. (92)

The students invariably find the plagiarized sentences readily and accurately. I then lead a brief discussion of the features that they used to identify the plagiarism. My students inform me that the vocabulary and the length and complexity of sentences are dead giveaways.

I then ask my students how much background and how many years of experience they have had in composition instruction. Obviously, they have had none. "So," I ask them, "if you can spot plagiarism without any formal training or experience, do you really think that I won't be able to catch you if you try to sneak somebody else's writing into your essay or report?"

This approach, this method of *showing* students, has been *much* more successful. Plagiarism still rears its ugly head on rare occasions, but not nearly as often as it used to. Whereas in many years of teaching, I had never before had a semester that was completely plagiarism free, I now have had several.

Receptive Knowledge

As previously noted, as students advance up the grade ladder, they are exposed to an ever-increasing amount of well-written material. This area of subconscious knowledge is a rich and useful one to tap into. Donohue (24) describes an essay-level activity that does just that. She suggests that you show students (I do it in small groups) examples of student writing that range from weak to strong, and then have them rank order the papers. Even though many of your students may not be able to produce strong papers, they will certainly be able to recognize them. Discuss the results, and come to a consensus rank ordering of the essays. Once the class is in agreement about the ordering, ask leading questions to help students discover parts of a well-written example that combine to make it successful: organization of ideas, supporting evidence, introduction, conclusion, voice, rhetorical devices, structural features, effective sentences, and so on. Using student papers to guide the class to consciously discern some of the characteristics of good writing is a powerful tool to use to help students acquire these same characteristics in their own writing.

Summary

This chapter examined the various parts of an essay (title, introduction, conclusion, and body) from the perspective of the role that each plays as the reader processes the text. It detailed ways to help your students in the following areas:

- **Introductions and conclusions.** We listed specific devices that students could use to create each, and outlined a way to help your students craft these important segments of a piece of writing.

- **Body.** We discussed the important role that variety plays in readers' minds, but also noted the critical role of consistency when it comes to topic maintenance, parallelism, and voice.

- **Writing process.** We outlined the order in which each of the components of an essay should be drafted.

- **Research paper.** We contrasted the typical school-based research paper with the probable rhetorical situations that your students will face in future years and suggested creating more realistic and challenging research classroom scenarios. We also explored an approach that will help you prevent plagiarism in your classes.

We ended the chapter with an activity that helps students verbalize and understand the components of a well-written essay in contrast to weaker ones.

Further Reading

For an excellent collection of activities and ideas regarding the writing of essays, see Kelly Gallagher's *Teaching Adolescent Writers*.

For an in-depth examination of genres as they apply to writing, see Deborah Dean's *Genre Theory*.

For more details on writing research papers for school versus in real life, see Randy Bomer's *Time for Meaning*.

For a beautifully laid out, detailed analysis and explanation of the I-Search paper with tips and examples, see "Writing an I-Search Paper."

8

Dialectically Diverse Writers

This chapter deals with an area of concern that many English language arts teachers around the country must deal with: how to close the achievement gap in writing for dialectically diverse students, that is, students who speak a so-called nonstandard version of English. These students are often referred to as Standard English learners or SELs. Many of them will be writing in future academic, business, and other professional worlds for the same audience as their "Standard" English-speaking counterparts, that is, for readers who, as a group, have similar demands, expectations, and processing skills. One of the expectations is that writers express themselves in Standard Written English, a variety of English that is at variance with some of the conventions that SELs employ. Therefore, SELs enter into the writing equation with more hurdles to clear than their Standard English-speaking counterparts have. However, SELs possess a vast storehouse of knowledge about English in their speaking brains that, if tapped into appropriately, can help them tremendously as they attempt to acquire Standard Written English skills.

We begin with a self-analysis tool designed to help you understand the parameters of the problems that teachers face when working with SELs. Then, to assist you in working with the speaking brains that all SELs have, I present guidelines and activities to help teachers understand and deal with many of the issues that SELs bring to the table.

Language Awareness

Most higher education programs for preservice English teachers concentrate heavily on the study of literature, giving the study of language short shrift. And yet graduates are expected to be the go-to people on campus for the development of areas that have little to do with literature per se: vocabulary acquisition, reading fluency, spelling, and writing. To further complicate matters, English teachers often have to work with English language learners (ELLs, or non-native speakers) and SELs in domains even further removed from things literary. How to teach writing to ELLs is beyond the scope of this book, but I will examine how to work with SELs in the writing classroom.

Before you can be expected to work effectively with SELs, you need a good understanding of dialects from both a linguistic and a social perspective. As Rebecca Wheeler and Rachel Swords note, "A linguistically informed language arts speaks not only to the structure of the language but also to our attitudes toward language in the classroom" (14). With that thought in mind, I have prepared a tool for you to use to self-assess your understanding of language and society.

Instructions and Survey

Read each statement and circle the number that best represents your honest reaction to it. These are not trick questions, so you don't need to look for traps. Just read each statement and react to it truthfully. After you have completed the twenty items, add up all of the numbers that you have circled, and write that total in the blank at the bottom of the survey. (You can, of course, write your responses on a separate sheet of paper and do the math there.) I will then give you my answer to each item and explain my reasoning, allowing you to compare your answers to mine and, where we differ, to see why our answers diverge.

Language Awareness Survey

1 = Strongly Agree 2 = Agree 3 = Neutral 4 = Disagree 5 = Strongly Disagree

1. One's language and one's race are closely interrelated.

    1   2   3   4   5

2. Your goal as an educator is to replace a student's nonstandard dialect with Standard English.

    1   2   3   4   5

3. Judgments about correct and incorrect language are linguistically based.

    1   2   3   4   5

4. There are English speakers who do not speak a dialect of English.

    1   2   3   4   5

5. Speakers of a nonstandard dialect process language differently than do speakers of Standard English.

    1   2   3   4   5

6. Standard English is more efficient than nonstandard English.

    1   2   3   4   5

7. Standard English is more logical than nonstandard English.

    1   2   3   4   5

8. The only significant components of one's conversational language are vocabulary and rules on pronunciation and grammar.

    1   2   3   4   5

9. Standard English is the correct way to speak at all times.

    1   2   3   4   5

10. There are national norms for acceptable communicative behavior within the United States.

    1   2   3   4   5

11. Educated people do not make judgments about an individual based on his or her language.

    1   2   3   4   5

12. In general, speaking a nonstandard dialect is indicative of low cognitive development.

    1   2   3   4   5

13. Standard English is more rule-based than are other dialects of English.

    1   2   3   4   5

14. Most standardized tests of English are based on rules of English used by individuals in all cultural groups.

    1   2   3   4   5

15. Speakers of African American Vernacular English (AAVE; also called Black English) choose not to follow Standard English rules because the speakers are lazy.

    1   2   3   4   5

16. In general, students from poor families do not communicate as well as those from middle- or upper-class families.

    1   2   3   4   5

17. Students who speak AAVE do not know grammar very well.

    1   2   3   4   5

18. Parents who do not speak Standard English should avoid talking to their children to prevent them from developing poor speech habits.

    1   2   3   4   5

19. In general, there is a relationship between the language of a child's home environment and his or her intelligence.

    1   2   3   4   5

20. Avoid nonstandard English in the classroom at all times because it will interfere with the acquisition of Standard English.

    1   2   3   4   5

Total: _____

Learning to Write for Readers: Using Brain-Based Strategies by John T. Crow © 2011 NCTE.

You should strongly disagree with every statement on the survey. Therefore, the closer your total comes to 100 points (20 □ 5), the deeper your understanding of how language and society interact.

I have given this survey to participants in workshops all over the United States. Most English language arts teachers I have worked with score between 60 and 80; rarely do I find someone who scores in the 90s. Let's look at each item to see why Strongly Disagree is the proper response across the board.

1. **One's language and one's race are closely interrelated.** Take a black baby and place her in the Queen of England's family, and that child will grow up speaking absolutely perfect Queen's English. Take a white baby and place him with a family in Harlem, and that child will grow up speaking absolutely perfect AAVE. Language and *cultural environment* are closely interrelated; language and race are not interrelated at all. While it's true that race can have a strong influence on one's culture, one's genetic makeup plays no role in the variety of language one acquires.

2. **Your goal as an educator is to replace a student's nonstandard dialect with Standard English.** Many students resent efforts to eliminate the language of their home environment, and will resist any attempt to do so. Their home or street language is a *register*, which *Merriam-Webster's* defines linguistically as "any of the varieties of a language that a speaker uses in a particular social context" ("Register"). This register communicates very well in students' out-of-school environment, so trying to eliminate it is nonsensical to them. For most SELs, this simply isn't going to happen. Your task is to give your students an *additional* register, a register that is not stigmatized in academic or business and professional circles—Standard English. Your job, therefore, is additive, not eradicative.

3. **Judgments about correct and incorrect language are linguistically based.** I grew up in the rural south. I was in college before I discovered, much to my amazement, that *seldomly* and *irregardless* were not words to a large segment of English speakers. In my home environment, saying things like "I seen her" or "I don't want none" would go unnoticed in many circles. However, such is certainly not the case in most corners of the English-speaking world: most people would look askance at me if I used these words or grammatical constructions. So the identical language can cause a wide range of reactions depending on the audience. Judgments about correctness of language are almost always *socially* based, not linguistically based. The language is not

wrong per se; in fact, I am certain that you, my reader, understood what I meant by each of my earlier examples. The problem arises because the register is wrong—the language is looked down upon in most social contexts.

4. **There are English speakers who do not speak a dialect of English.** Everybody speaks a dialect. Standard English is just as much a dialect of English as AAVE, or the English of the Deep South, or the English of Bostonians, or . . .

5. **Speakers of a nonstandard dialect process language differently than do speakers of Standard English.** The brain, the machine for processing language, functions exactly the same for nonstandard speakers as for Standard speakers. It's programmed a bit differently, but it processes language in exactly the same manner.

6. **Standard English is more efficient than nonstandard English.** Every dialect of every language evolves to meet the needs of the community of speakers it serves. Nonstandard English is every bit as efficient a tool for communication in its community of speakers as Standard English is in its community.

7. **Standard English is more logical than nonstandard English.** Nonstandard English is just as logical as its standard counterpart. In fact, from a position of pure logic, nonstandard English can sometimes appear to be *more* logical. For example, what does the -s suffix mean in a sentence such as "He eats"? It indicates that the subject of the verb is third-person singular. But by definition, "He" is third-person singular, so that fact has already been established. From a logical perspective, then, the -s suffix is redundant. Some nonstandard dialects drop this -s as a way to streamline the language. Which version is more *logical*?

8. **The only significant components of one's conversational language are vocabulary and rules on pronunciation and grammar.** Components such as nonverbal gestures, facial expressions, eye contact, space between speakers, volume, speed, and so on can have a profound effect on one's understanding. For example, if you were aware of nothing but a speaker's vocabulary, pronunciation, and grammar, you would not be able to make judgments about things such as truth value or emotional state of the speaker. These components cause misunderstandings that often occur beyond conscious awareness, and their effects can be devastating.

9. **Standard English is the correct way to speak at all times.** Standard English can be the wrong register to use just as readily as can nonstandard English. I live in central Florida in a neighborhood of people who, like myself, are of modest means. What would my neighbor think of me if I were to ask him, "To whom are you speaking?" Much more acceptable would be something like "Who're you talkin' to?" or "You talkin' to me?" Using my teaching register, something more closely resembling Standard English, would not be well received in my neighborhood. My rural southern register is a much better fit.

10. **There are national norms for acceptable communicative behavior within the United States.** Acceptable communicative behavior differs from community to community, from area to area. Standard English is certainly judged as proper in many social settings, but is it a national norm? Absolutely not. In fact, Standard English itself will vary from geographical area to geographical area.

11. **Educated people do not make judgments about an individual based on his or her language.** One could correctly state that educated people *should not* make judgments based on a person's language, but to say that they *do not* is preposterous. Judging a person's background, education level, competency, and so on by the language she speaks is an ineradicable component of human behavior irrespective of educational levels. Though we, as English teachers, should be accepting of nonstandard dialects, we do our students a great disservice if we fail to help them acquire a more broadly accepted standard register.

12. **In general, speaking a nonstandard dialect is indicative of low cognitive development.** Children acquire nonstandard English from exposure to the language around them in the identical way that children acquire Standard English. Although language development goes hand in hand with cognitive development, the variety of language that is acquired neither impedes nor facilitates general cognitive development.

13. **Standard English is more rule-based than are other dialects of English.** Every dialect is systematic and rule-governed. Language becomes intelligible to a group of people only when it follows a set of rules that everyone has mastered. A listener may feel that AAVE, for example, has no rules because it violates some of his or her own internalized rules. But AAVE is just as fundamentally rule-governed as any other dialect of English. An article in an

August 1972 edition of *Time* ("Education") summed the situation up nicely: "Frequently when Black English sounds ungrammatical to white ears, it is merely conforming to its own rules."

14. **Most standardized tests of English are based on rules of English used by individuals in all cultural groups.** This is patently false. Most standardized tests of English are based on Standard English rules. Children who, by accident of birth, grew up in a community of nonstandard English speakers are at an immediate disadvantage. They have additional barriers to overcome before they can do as well as children who, again by accident of birth, grew up in a community of Standard English speakers.

15. **Speakers of AAVE choose not to follow Standard English rules because the speakers are lazy.** Unfortunately, this is a commonly held misconception. Speakers of AAVE acquired their language from the community of speakers that surrounded them, just as standard-English-speaking children did. John Rickford notes that AAVE is "no more lazy English than Italian is lazy Latin" (qtd. in Redd and Webb 5).

16. **In general, students from poor families do not communicate as well as those from middle- or upper-class families.** Children from poor families are more likely to be born into an environment where literacy skills are traditionally weak or undervalued. As a result, they develop a strong oral tradition. They become marvelously inventive speakers within their own dialects. They may struggle when trying to express themselves in situations where Standard English is required, but such is not the case on the street or at home.

17. **Students who speak AAVE do not know grammar very well.** Students who speak AAVE are absolute masters of the grammar of AAVE. Otherwise, they wouldn't be able to communicate with each other. Further, the grammar of AAVE is identical to the grammar of Standard English far more often than it is different. Although the differences may be jarring, they are only a small part of the overall picture.

18. **Parents who do not speak Standard English should avoid talking to their children to prevent them from developing poor speech habits.** This one is about as silly as it gets. If you really want to interfere with the speech development of your children, avoid talking to them. Children have a miraculous facility for self-adjustment as far as language is concerned. They will

acquire the language they need to communicate from the various groups with whom they interact. The key requirement in language acquisition is interaction with other speakers.

19. **In general, there is a relationship between the language of a child's home environment and his or her intelligence.** Research has shown over and over that one's native dialect or language has no correlation whatsoever to intelligence. In fact, children who are found to be mentally challenged usually acquire good native control over the spoken language of their environment. (Complete failure to develop language skills is a hallmark of profound mental retardation.) Language acquisition is a reflection of one's cultural environment, not one's intelligence (except at the extreme ends of the intelligence scale).

20. **Avoid nonstandard English in the classroom at all times because it will interfere with the acquisition of Standard English.** Not true at all. In fact, handled properly, nonstandard English can be a powerful ally in developing Standard English skills. I will develop this concept in the remainder of this chapter.

Closing the Achievement Gap in Writing

Labeling and Code Switching

As the previous discussion supports, our goal while working with SELs is to persuade them that Standard English is a useful tool for them, and then to help them master it. Before we can make much progress toward that goal, we have to disabuse ourselves of the notion that Standard English is a superior form of English and that any other dialect of English is a corruption. Teresa Redd and Karen Webb address the issue:

> Dialects are variations of a language that are mutually intelligible but include some grammatical and/or pronunciation patterns that are unique to speakers in certain regions, social classes, or ethnic groups....Thus, even Standard American English is a dialect....Yet much of the public wrongly assumes that the standard dialect is the English language because it is the dialect promoted by the people in power. (8)

The traditional approach to working with nonstandard English is to frown on it, label it as wrong, or brand it as some lower form of communication. And in doing so, we English teachers have been shooting ourselves in the collective foot for decades.

Dennis Baron makes the following plea: we should "transmute the conventional right-wrong language dichotomy into a contextually-dependent sliding scale of language that works in particular situations, and language that may not work so well, demonstrating that there are many varieties of standard English, not just one." Research shows us repeatedly that if we truly want to help SELs to acquire Standard English, we should respect their home language, take advantage of what they already know, and build from there.

To close the achievement gap in writing, we must accept the various versions of nonstandard English as fully formed, rule-governed, logical derivatives of English that are spoken by a community of intelligent, capable individuals. Rather than try to drive it out of the classroom, let students know that you appreciate its role in their lives, but that your job is to help them acquire another way of speaking and writing, a way that will remove barriers and help them succeed in academic and business or professional circles. Start by working with your students to establish labels for the two general types of language:

- Home or street or *informal*: the language that students use outside the classroom to talk to friends, family members, and others
- School or *formal*: the language that you are targeting in the classroom

Following Wheeler and Swords's lead, I'll use informal and formal to label the two varieties (21). At the risk of repeating myself, be sure students understand that you are working with formal English, not because it's better than or superior to informal English, but because they will benefit from being able to speak and write formal English in many areas of their future lives.

Once you have the two types of language discussed and named, *never* refer to informal English as wrong or nonstandard. If students use nonstandard English in your classroom when speaking or writing, tell them that they are using informal language (or whatever name you have established) and remind them that, in your class, you are helping them to learn another way to speak or write. Then ask students if they can say or write the same utterance in formal English. If they struggle, ask other students to help them. With patience, acceptance, and gentle guidance, students will begin to recognize informal English when they hear or use it, and will know how to change to a more formal variety when the situation requires it. The ability to change forms of a language according to one's audience is called *code switching*. All of your students code switch regularly: they change how they speak when talking to you, to their friends, to their parents, to their religious leaders, and so on. Once again, we are tapping into and leveraging a body of knowledge in their subconscious speaking brains. The act itself isn't new to them; the conscious awareness and the label for the act are. Once they understand the concept of code switching, this phenomenon becomes a powerful ally in the writing classroom. Constance Weaver sees writing as the perfect place for code-switching activities:

> Speakers of a nonmainstream dialect . . . are understandably reluctant to accept the idea that their language variety may not be acceptable in all life situations; indeed, they may resent the school's apparent rejection of their home or peer language and resist attempts to help them code-switch to standard features. Teaching such code-switching as part of editing is perhaps the least threatening, least resistance-generating way to approach it: After all, everybody needs to edit. (145)

In the Classroom

Once your students understand what you are trying to accomplish, several activities are available to help you guide them to writing that is not stigmatized, to writing that better meets the expectations of their future readers.

Classroom Activity: Damage Control

As SELs progress up the grade ladder, they are often criticized by various teachers because of their perceived language inabilities. The damage caused by these rebukes can accrue across time and seriously interfere with your efforts to improve your students' writing ability. Before significant progress can be made, this damage must be dealt with directly. Randy Bomer recommends the following:

> Especially with mature students, I spend several days of class time letting them critique the damage that has been done to their self-concept as readers and writers. . . . I try to help them understand that the problem is not inside them, in the way their brain is constructed or their native intelligence, but in the experiences they recall when they write about the pain or confusion they have felt in school. (21)

For a real eye-opener, a true window into the harm that might have been done by writing teachers in your students' past, I strongly encourage you to try

Bomer's suggestion: ask your students to write candidly about their experience with writing in past classes. Bomer notes that "neither this book nor any other could ever be so damning an indictment of traditional literacy instruction, or so urgent and inspiring a call to change, as a wad of letters written by a roomful of second-semester seniors in response to the question, What has your life history as a writer been like?" (21). Following Bomer's recommendation, I ask my students to respond to this question as an initial writing activity (not for a grade, of course) in every writing class I teach. The results have helped me to see some of the things I was doing that were less than helpful, and have given me valuable insights into what I need to do to start improving my effectiveness. I heartily recommend this activity.

Classroom Activity: Flip the Switch

As we noted earlier, in the writing classroom, your job is to help your SELs acquire another register—Standard English. You want to instill in your SELs a sense of pride in their ability to speak and understand their informal dialect—something that you, their teacher, may not be able to do as well, if at all. Use this body of knowledge that they possess to help them acquire a Standard English register. Kristen Turner describes an outstanding activity that will go a long way toward accomplishing this goal. She calls this activity "Flip the Switch." The activity (with some minor modifications) goes as follows:

- Ask students to brainstorm a list of environments where they change their language according to their audience (that is, switch to a different register). Examples might include at home with parents, in the classroom with teachers, on the street with best friends, during job interviews, while texting, and so on.

- Select three registers from the student-generated list and add formal English as a fourth version. Create a table with four columns, each headed with the three selected register names plus formal English.

- Provide a sentence (or sentences) suitable for one of the categories. For example, you might start with "Good morning. How are you?"

- Ask students to put your sentence into its proper column (or columns—the same utterance might be used in more than one register). Then ask them to flip the switch—that is, to complete the table by translating the language into the other registers. See Table 8.1 for a possible version. (Forgive me if Version 3 has changed by the time you read this!)

TABLE 8.1. Flip the Switch Example

Version 1 Texting	Version 2 Teacher	Version 3 Friend	Formal English
hey how r u?	Good morning. How are you?	Yo, what's goin' on?	Good morning. How are you?

- Now add a row to the table, and ask students to provide an utterance that goes into one of the empty cells. Then ask them to flip the switch. Repeat, occasionally changing the headings (the registers) except for formal English.

- On another day, revisit the activity by dividing the class into small groups. Ask each group to come up with one sentence, place it in a table of their making, and handle the switch flipping. Share the results with the class.

- Show students a list of possible registers. Ask student A to come up with a sentence and then challenge another student, student B, to flip the switch to a specific register that student A selects. Be sure to always include formal English in your activity.

- You, the teacher, may not be able to flip the switch in many situations— that's great! Join your students in the previous exercise: tell your class that you are going to be student B. Their job is to come up with formal English utterances and challenge you to flip the switch to a register of their choosing. In this manner, you can learn from your students, celebrate what they know, and build from there. Handled properly, it's a lot of fun for both you and your students.

In my classrooms, once students understand this activity, I find myself using Flip the Switch often in my daily teaching:

- **Oral language.** Suppose that a student says, "I done it" during class. At first, I might say something like, "That's informal English. Remember that we are practicing formal English in this class. How would you say that in formal English?" Later on, all I have to say in response is, "Flip the switch." My students know exactly what to do.

- **Written language.** If, during conferences, I see that a student has written a slang expression, a regionalism, or a grammatical feature that comes from his or her informal English, I point to it and simply say, "Flip the switch." If marking the paper, I write "F/S" above the informal language and ask the student to change it for me.

Contrastive Analysis

Remember that nonstandard dialects are logical, rule-governed systems. Therefore, anything you hear or see that is at variance with Standard English grammar has a basis in an established rule of that nonstandard dialect. Your teaching efficiency will improve if you can determine what the underlying rule is, and then use it as a springboard to the formal English version. Linguists use the term *contrastive analysis* to label the process of comparing one language, dialect, or register with another in order to figure out the underlying rules. When working with SELs, contrastive analysis is a powerful tool to use.

Contrastive Analysis for Teachers

Gather samples of informal English utterances that are at variance with formal English, and put them in a table beside their formal English counterparts. (You may need to ask some of your SELs to help you understand exactly what is meant by one version versus the other.) Then look for patterns of informal utterances that seem to violate the same rule in formal English. Contrast the two sets of utterances to try to derive the underlying rule for the informal version. Once you think you have it, try it out with some of your SELs to see if it works. If you can capture the underlying rule, you'll be much better equipped to find more effective ways to present the distinction to your students as you help them in their acquisition of formal English writing. I suggest that you examine Wheeler and Swords's excellent book *Code-Switching*. The authors devote six chapters to the contrastive analyses of Standard English and common informal English patterns and then apply the results to the classroom.

If you are working primarily with speakers of AAVE, Wikipedia has a thorough, carefully researched page devoted to an analysis of the features of this dialect ("African American Vernacular English"). The overview contains both linguistic terminology and plain English examples and explanations, along with a wealth of additional links and printed resources that will help you appreciate the rules that underlie AAVE.

Classroom Activity: Contrastive Analysis for Students

Once you understand the underlying rule (or rules) for a specific feature that you want to work on, you can create an inquiry-based activity that allows SELs to contrast informal and formal English versions to see if they can derive how to change a targeted informal English feature into formal English. The following is an example of an inquiry-based lesson working with a feature of AAVE: progressive verb formation in the present tense.

- Find out the rule. Look at the contrasting examples in Table 8.2 and decide the rule that underlies AAVE utterances.

- Once you have figured out the rule, create a table of contrasting sentences for students to examine. (Table 8.2 is an example.)

- Create a list of questions to guide students in their analysis.

   1. When are all of these things happening?

      a. Yesterday

      b. Right now

      c. Tomorrow

   2. When formal English talks about something that is happening right now, it differs in two ways from informal English:

      a. In informal English, one letter is dropped. What is that letter?

      b. In informal English, one word is dropped, but it is not always the same word. List the words that are added in formal English.

   3. All of the words that are added on the formal side come from a single basic form. The following two sentences will show you the basic form. What is it?

TABLE 8.2. Sentences to Analyze

Sentence #		Informal	Formal
	1.	He goin' to town.	He is going to town.
	2.	John doin' his homework.	John is doing his homework.
	3.	My mom cookin' dinner.	My mom is cooking dinner.
	4.	We lookin' for someone.	We are looking for someone.
	5.	I walkin' to school.	I am walking to school.

a. He is rich.

b. He wants _____ rich.

4. How do you know which form of this added word to use in formal English?

5. When writing, if you want to quote somebody who is speaking informal English, how do you show that the person is dropping the -*g*?

6. You now have enough information to be able to figure out how to flip the switch from informal to formal English in situations like this. So when formal English talks about something that is happening right now, it differs from informal English in two ways:

a. _____

b. _____

As you work through this exercise (and others like it), you need to keep several points in mind:

- SELs have been exposed to formal English in professionally written material that they read, in movies, on television, and from formal English speakers. So, unlike working on a foreign language, the areas that you target will not be new to them. This exposure will create triple-X knowledge in their brains, waiting for you to take advantage of it.

- Notice that, for example, question 2 in the previous list contains the answer to question 1. No problem: this is not a test. It's an exercise to help students understand the teaching point.

- Students may not always be able to answer all of the questions. Again, no problem: being challenged by problem-solving situations creates teachable moments that enhance retention.

- You can do these types of inquiry-based analyses together as a class, in small groups, or individually.

If you choose to do the exercise in small groups or individually, then you will need to compare answers and discuss the targeted feature, ensuring that you answer all of the questions in the process. Once you have completed all the steps in this activity, you can do an exercise or two that manipulates the teaching point. But from this point forward, *never allow your students to use the informal version*, whether speaking or writing, in your class. Remember: right or wrong is not the issue here. You are not correcting the students; you are asking them to change to a different register, to flip the switch.

Summary

This chapter began with a self-assessment survey and discussion designed to help English language arts teachers reach a common understanding of nonstandard dialects. I then introduced and examined the following:

- **Register:** a variety of a language that a speaker uses in a social context.
- **Labeling:** the necessity of naming two registers: (1) the nonstandard dialect(s) that your students speak and (2) Standard English.
- **Code switching:** the ability to change registers according to one's audience.
- **Flip the switch:** activities that have students "translating" from nonstandard English into Standard English or vice versa.
- **Contrastive analysis:** the determination of the rules that govern a nonstandard dialect by contrasting samples from it with their corresponding Standard English versions.

Further Reading

For excellent general coverage of how to help dialectically diverse writers acquire Standard English, see *Code-Switching* by Rebecca Wheeler and Rachel Swords.

For an analysis of code switching as it applies to grammar, see David Brown's *In Other Words*.

For detailed coverage of code-switching activities for elementary children, see Wheeler and Swords's *Code-Switching Lessons*.

For a truly interesting, eye-opening look at Standard versus nonstandard English and the roles they play in our society, see Rosina Lippi-Green's *English with an Accent*.

PARIS

IN THE

THE SPRING

Appendix B: Textual Analysis Worksheet

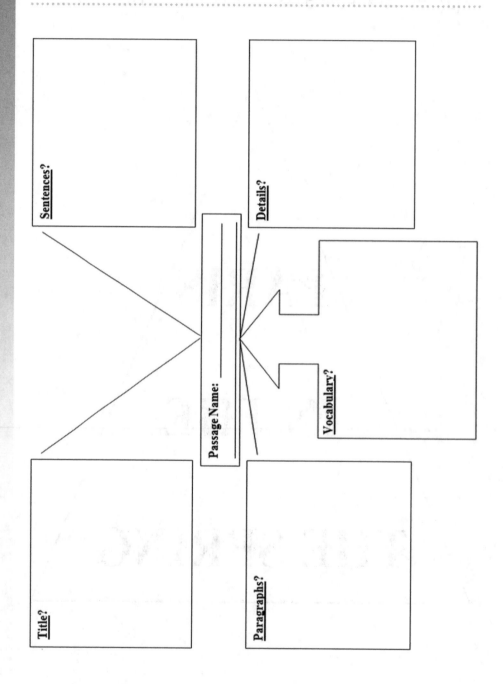

Sentences?

Details?

Passage Name: _____

Vocabulary?

Title?

Paragraphs?

Appendix C: Sentence Linkage Worksheet

Sentence Number	Source	Word or Phrase	#	New Topic	Method
1	☐ Topic ☐ Comment		2		☐ Repeated ☐ Derived
2	☐ Topic ☐ Comment		3		☐ Repeated ☐ Derived
3	☐ Topic ☐ Comment		4		☐ Repeated ☐ Derived
4	☐ Topic ☐ Comment		5		☐ Repeated ☐ Derived
5	☐ Topic ☐ Comment		6		☐ Repeated ☐ Derived
6	☐ Topic ☐ Comment		7		☐ Repeated ☐ Derived
7	☐ Topic ☐ Comment		8		☐ Repeated ☐ Derived
8	☐ Topic ☐ Comment		9		☐ Repeated ☐ Derived
9	☐ Topic ☐ Comment		10		☐ Repeated ☐ Derived
10	☐ Topic ☐ Comment		11		☐ Repeated ☐ Derived

Works Cited

"African American Vernacular English." *Wikipedia*. 7 Sept. 2010. Web. 12 Sept. 2010.

Anderson, Jeff. *Everyday Editing: Inviting Students to Develop Skill and Craft in Writer's Workshop*. Portland, ME: Stenhouse, 2007. Print.

Angelou, Maya. "New Directions." *Wouldn't Take Nothing for My Journey Now*. New York: Random House, 1993. 19–24. Print.

Baddeley, Alan, Michael W. Eysenck, and Michael C. Anderson. *Memory*. New York: Psychology Press, 2009. Print.

Baker, Jack Raymond, and Allen Brizee. "Genre and the Research Paper." *Purdue Online Writing Lab*. 17 Apr. 2010. Web. 26 Aug. 2010.

Baron, Dennis. "Language Lessons: It's Time for English Teachers to Stop Teaching That the Earth is Flat." *The Web of Language*. 1 Dec. 2009. Web. 4 Dec. 2009.

Berger, Kathleen Stassen. *The Developing Person through Childhood and Adolescence*. 7th ed. New York: Worth, 2005. Print.

Birkerts, Sven. "Into the Electronic Millennium." DiYanni 89–99.

Bollinger, R. Randal, et al. "Biofilms in the Large Bowel Suggest an Apparent Function of the Human Vermiform Appendix." *Journal of Theoretical Biology* 249.4 (2007): 826–31. Print.

Bomer, Randy. *Time for Meaning: Crafting Literate Lives in Middle and High School*. Portsmouth, NH: Heinemann, 1995. Print.

Bransford, John D. *Human Cognition: Learning, Understanding and Remembering*. Belmont, CA: Wadsworth, 1979. Print.

Bransford, John D., and Marcia K. Johnson. "Contextual Prerequisites for Understanding: Some Investigations of Comprehension and Recall." *Journal of Verbal Learning and Verbal Behavior* 11 (1972): 717–26. Print.

Brown, David West. *In Other Words: Lessons on Grammar, Code-Switching, and Academic Writing*. Portsmouth, NH: Heinemann, 2009. Print.

Carnegie Council on Advancing Adolescent Literacy. *Time to Act: An Agenda for Advancing Adolescent Literacy for College and Career Success*. New York: Carnegie, 2010. *Carnegie*. Web. 17 Sept. 2009.

Carrell, Patricia L. "Some Causes of Text-Boundedness and Schema Interference in ESL Reading." *Interactive Approaches to Second Language Reading*. Ed. Patricia L. Carrell,

Joann Devine, and David E. Eskey. Cambridge, UK: Cambridge UP, 1988. 101–13. Print.

Christensen, Francis, and Bonniejean Christensen. *Notes toward a New Rhetoric: Nine Essays for Teachers*. Ed. Don Stewart. 3rd ed. Bangor, ME: Booklocker.com, 2007. Print.

"Conclusions." *Handouts and Links*. The Writing Center, U of North Carolina at Chapel Hill, n.d. Web. 22 Dec. 2009.

Covey, Stephen R. *"The Seven Habits of Highly Effective People*: Habit Two: Begin with the End in Mind." *Stephencovey.com*. Web. 30 Dec. 2009.

Crow, John T. "Feeding Reading: Writing from an Information-Processing Perspective." *English Journal* 94.4 (2005): 45–51. Print.

———. *Unleashing Your Language Wizards: A Brain-Based Approach to Effective Editing and Writing*. Boston: Pearson, 2010. Print.

Dean, Deborah. *Genre Theory: Teaching, Writing, and Being*. Urbana, IL: NCTE, 2008. Print.

———. *Strategic Writing: The Writing Process and Beyond in the Secondary English Classroom*. Urbana, IL: NCTE, 2006. Print.

Dehaene, Stanislas. *Reading in the Brain: The Science and Evolution of a Human Invention*. New York: Viking, 2009. Print.

———. "Your Brain on Books." *Scientific American* 17 Nov. 2009. Web. 21 Nov. 2009.

Dickens, Charles. *A Tale of Two Cities*. New York: MacMillan, 1922. *Google Books*. Web. 2 Jan. 2010.

Dillard, Annie. "Heaven and Earth in Jest." DiYanni 169–72.

DiYanni, Robert, ed. *One Hundred Great Essays*. 4th ed. New York: Longman, 2011. Print.

Donohue, Lisa. *The Write Beginning: Instruction That Starts with the End in Mind and Guides Students to Become More Effective Writers*. Markham, Ont., Canada: Pembroke. 2009. Print.

"Education: Black English." *Time* 7 Aug. 1972. Web. 7 Sept. 2010.

Elias, Maurice J., et al. *Promoting Social and Emotional Learning: Guidelines for Educators*. Alexandria, VA: ASCD, 1997. Print.

Eysenck, Michael W. *Psychology: An International Perspective*. New York: Psychology Press, 2004. Print.

Fish, Stanley. "Devoid of Content." Editorial. *New York Times* 31 May 2005. Web. 7 Oct. 2008.

———. "What Should Colleges Teach? Part 2." Editorial. *New York Times* 31 Aug. 2009. Web. 2 Sept. 2009.

Fisher, Douglas, and Nancy Frey. *Background Knowledge: The Missing Piece of the Comprehension Puzzle*. Portsmouth, NH: Heinemann, 2009. Print.

Gallagher, Kelly. *Teaching Adolescent Writers*. Portland, ME: Stenhouse, 2006. Print.

Gerosa Bellos, Melina. "Galapagos Islands Vacation," Grade 7 FCAT 2.0 Reading Sample Questions, Sample 7. *Florida Comprehensive Assessment Test*. Tallahassee: Florida Department of Education, 2010. 1–16. *Florida Comprehensive Achievement Test*. Web. 11 July 2011.

Goodman, Kenneth S. "Reading: A Psycholinguistic Guessing Game." *Journal of the Reading Specialist* 6 (1967): 126–35. Print.

Gorman, Christine, et al. "The New Science of Dyslexia." *Time* 28 July 2003. Web. 28 Aug. 2009.

Grazulis, Thomas P. *The Tornado: Nature's Ultimate Windstorm*. Norman: U of Oklahoma P, 2003. Print.

Greene, Stuart. "Exploring the Relationship between Authorship and Reading." *Hearing Ourselves Think: Cognitive Research in the College Writing Classroom*. Ed. Ann M. Penrose and Barbara M. Sitko. New York: Oxford UP, 1993. 33–51. Print.

Hale, Elizabeth. *Crafting Writers, K–6*. Portland, ME: Stenhouse, 2008. Print.

Harley, Trevor A. *The Psychology of Language: From Data to Theory*. 3rd ed. New York: Psychology Press, 2008. Print.

"Huge Bones Make Big Hit." *Texas Assessment of Knowledge and Skills: Grade 4: Writing, Mathematics, Reading*. Austin: Texas Education Agency, 2003. 57–64. *Texas Education Agency*. Web. 12 Aug. 2009.

Jensen, Eric. *Brain-Based Learning: The New Paradigm of Teaching*. 2nd ed. Thousand Oaks, CA: Corwin, 2008. Print.

Kolln, Martha. *Rhetorical Grammar: Grammatical Choices, Rhetorical Effects*. 4th ed. New York: Longman, 2003. Print.

Kozol, Jonathan. "The Human Cost of an Illiterate Society." *Illiterate America*. By Kozol. Garden City, NY: Anchor/Doubleday, 1985. 22–29. Web. 13 Apr. 2010.

Lindblom, Ken. "From the Editor." *English Journal* 99.6 (2010): 14–16. Print.

———. "From the Editor," *English Journal* 100.4 (2011): 10–11. Print.

Lippi-Green, Rosina. *English with an Accent: Language, Ideology, and Discrimination in the United States*. London: Routledge, 1997. Print.

Rev. of *The Loss of a Teardrop Diamond*. Dir. Jodie Markell. *Movie Review Query Engine*. Web. 30 Dec. 2009.

London, Jack. *Call of the Wild*. 1903. *The Jack London Online Collection*. Sonoma State U. Web. 23 Aug. 2010.

Miller, Barbara. "Scientists Discover True Function of Appendix Organ." *ABC News*. 10 Oct. 2007. Web. 22 Mar. 2010.

Miller, George A. "The Magical Number Seven, Plus or Minus Two: Some Limits on Our Capacity for Processing Information." *Psychological Review* 63 (1956): 81–97. Print.

National Commission on Writing in America's Schools and Colleges. *The Neglected "R": The Need for a Writing Revolution*. Reston, VA: College Board, Apr. 2003. *College Board*. Web. 27 Aug. 2009.

———. *Writing: A Ticket to Work . . . Or a Ticket Out: A Survey of Business Leaders*. Reston, VA: College Board, Sept. 2004. *College Board*. Web. 27 Aug. 2009.

Overmeyer, Mark. *What Student Writing Teaches Us: Formative Assessment in the Writing Workshop*. Portland, ME: Stenhouse, 2009. Print.

Perera, Katherine. "The Language Demands of School Learning." *Linguistics and the Teacher*. Ed. Ronald Carter. London: Routledge and Kegan Paul, 1982. 114–36. Print.

Reber, Paul. "What Is the Memory Capacity of the Human Brain?" *Scientific American* 19 Apr. 2010. Web. 22 Apr. 2010.

Redd, Teresa M., and Karen Schuster Webb. *A Teacher's Introduction to African American English: What a Writing Teacher Should Know*. Urbana, IL: NCTE, 2005. Print.

"Register." *Merriam-Webster.com*. Web. 29 Aug. 2010.

"The Rhetorical Situation," *Purdue Online Writing Lab*. Web. 29 July 2011.

"Schema." *WordNet Search 3.1*. Web. 30 Aug. 2009.

Schuster, Edgar H. *Breaking the Rules: Liberating Writers through Innovative Grammar Instruction*. Portsmouth, NH: Heinemann, 2003. Print.

"Scope Creep." *Business Dictionary.com*. Web. 24 Aug. 2009.

Simon, Seymour. "The Gray Whale in Winter." *WASL—Washington Assessment of Student Learning: Using Results to Improve Student Learning, Reading Grade 4*. Olympia: State of Washington, Office of the Superintendent of Public Instruction.10 Aug. 2004. 14–37. Web. 1 Apr. 2010.

"Social Insects." Practice Test. *Fourth Grade Reading Florida Comprehensive Assessment Test*. Tampa: U of South Florida, 2002. *FCAT Express*. Web. 30 Dec. 2009.

Sohn, Emily. "What the Appendix Is Good For." *Science News for Kids* 17 Mar. 2010. Web. 22 Mar 2010.

Spatt, Brenda. *Writing from Sources*. 6th ed. Boston: Bedford/St. Martin's, 2003. Print.

Strunk, William, Jr., and E. B. White. *The Elements of Style*. 4th ed. New York: Longman, 2000. Print.

Talusan, Meredith, and Janice Chen. "Demos of Lightness Illusions." *Perceptual Science Group, MIT*. Web. 12 Sept. 2009.

Tan, Amy. "Mother Tongue." *The Short Prose Reader*. Ed. Gilbert H. Muller and Harvey S. Wiener. 9th ed. Boston: McGraw-Hill, 2000. 27–37. Print.

Turner, Kristen Hawley. "Flipping the Switch: Code-Switching from Text Speak to Standard English." *English Journal* 98.5 (2009): 60–65. Print.

Walsh, Bryan. "Decoding the Tasmanian Devil's Deadly Cancer." *Time* 1 Jan. 2010. Web. 1 Jan. 2010.

Weaver, Constance. *Grammar to Enrich and Enhance Writing*. Portsmouth, NH: Heinemann, 2008. Print.

Wheeler, Rebecca S., and Rachel Swords. *Code-Switching Lessons: Grammar Strategies for Linguistically Diverse Writers*. Portsmouth, NH: Heinemann, 2010. Print.

———. *Code-Switching: Teaching Standard English in Urban Classrooms*. Urbana, IL: NCTE, 2006. Print.

Willingham, Daniel T. *Why Don't Students Like School? A Cognitive Scientist Answers Questions about How the Mind Works and What It Means for the Classroom*. San Francisco: Jossey-Bass, 2009. Print.

"Writing an I-Search Paper." *Writing Workshop*. Web. 25 Aug. 2010.

Index

African American Vernacular English (AAVE), 129–33

Analyzing text, 59–68

Anderson, J., 81

Angelou, M., 60

Appositives, 17–18

Audience, 28, 29, 68–75
    thinking about, 28, 29
    tailoring writing to, 68–75

Background knowledge, 31–37, 58

Baker, J., 122

Baron, D., 135

Berger, K., 20

Body, of essay, 116–19

Bomer, R., 121, 125

Brain function
    importance of understanding, xiii–xiv, 1
    of readers, xiii
    self-googling, 20–22, 110
    of students, xiv
    of teachers, xiv

Brizee, A., 122

Brown, D., 88, 91

Carmichael, L., 31

Carnegie Council on Advancing Literacy, xi, xii

Carrell, P., 21

Chen, J., 33

Christensen, B., 64

Christensen, F., 64

Chunking, 28–31

Classroom activities and demonstrations
    Background Knowledge and Memory, 31–33
    Bad Introduction, 43–45
    Change the Audience, 71
    Changing Audiences, 26–27
    Chunking, 28–31
    Contrastive Analysis for Students, 140–41
    Contrast the Audience, 71–75
    Damage Control, 136–37
    Do What?, 47–48
    Erroneous Prediction, 5–6
    Eye Movement, 2–3
    Five Words in a Sentence, 80–81
    Flip the Switch, 137–39
    Good Introduction, 45–46
    GUESS Errors, 10
    GUESS from the Introduction, 46
    GUESS Signals, 52–55
    GUESS the Audience, 68–71
    Humans versus Computers Part IA, 21–22
    Humans versus Computers Part IB, 22
    Humans versus Computers Part II, 23–24
    Inadequate Definition of *Paragraph*, 95–98
    Inadequate Definition of *Sentence*, 78–80
    Inferences, 25–26
    Known-New Contract, 86–87
    Mining Paragraphs, 103–4
    Mining Texts, 60–63

Missing Pieces, 110–12
Multi-Paragraph Topic Maintenance, 99–102
Name That Sentence, 83–86
Optical Illusion, 33–37
Professional GUESSing, 7–8
Reconstructing Transitions, 14–17
Round-Robin Writing, 13
Says–Does, 65–66
Sentence Spotlight, 81–82
Student GUESSing, 8–10
Text-Mining Competition, 63–65
Text-Mining Logs, 65
Thinking about Audience, 28, 29
Title Insurance, 42
Topic-Comment Connections, 87–89
Two Types of Scope Creep, 105–7
Word for Word 1, 3–4
Word for Word 2, 5
Writing Logs, 66–68
Cognitive economy, 20
Colon, 54–55
Comma, 53, 64
Conclusion, of essay, 115
Consistency, 117–18
Contrastive analysis, 139–41
Covey, S., 120
Cultural environment, role in language, 130

Dash, 55
Dean, D., xii, 65, 66, 121, 125
Dehaene, S., 6
Dialectically diverse writers, 126–42
    closing achievement gap for, 134–39
    contrastive analysis and, 139–41
    language awareness and, 127–34
Dillard, A., 90
Donohue, L., 109, 124

Economy of effort, 20, 33–39
    optical illusions and, 33–37
    writing and, 37–39
Essays, 41–57, 109–25
    blueprint for, 119–20
    body, 116–19

conclusion, 115
    introduction, 42–46, 110–15
    plagiarism and, 123–4
    punctuation, 52–56
    reader expectations and, 41–57
    receptive knowledge and, 124
    research papers and, 121–23
    title, 241–42, 110–12
    topic sentence and thesis statement, 46–48
    transitions, 48–52
Exclamation point, 53
Experience, 58
Exploration, 58
Exposure, 58
Eye movement, during reading, 2–3

Fish, S., 77, 80, 109
Fonts, 52

Gallagher, K., xii, 125
Genre, defined, 121
Goodman, K., 19
Gradual release of control approach, 16
Greene, S., 16, 60
GUESS errors, 7–14, 91
    disjointed GUESS, 43
    at paragraph level, 98–104
    in peer evaluations, 10–12
    underprepared GUESS, 53

Hale, E., 59, 76, 83, 85
Hogan, H. P., 31

Inferences, 24, 25–27
Introduction, 43–46, 110–15
    devices for, 113–14
I-search papers, 122–23

Jensen, E., xv

Known-new contract, 86–87
Kozol, J., 87, 88

Language awareness, 127–34
    survey, 128–34

Lindblom, K., 119

Memory, 28, 31–33
    background knowledge and, 31–33
    short-term, 28
Mining texts, 60–68

National Commission on Writing in
    America's Schools and Colleges, xi
Nonfiction, categories of, 121

Optical illusions, 33–37
Oral language, 138

Paragraphs, 94–108
    definitions of, 94–98
    GUESS errors and, 98–104
    multi-paragraph topic maintenance,
        98–104
    scope creep and, 104–7
Parallelism, 117
Parentheses, 55
Perera, K., xiii
Period (punctuation), 53
Plagiarism, 123–24
Punctuation, 52–56

Question mark, 53–54

Reader expectations, essay form and,
    41–57
Reading
    eye movement during, 2–3
    feeding, 1–18
    like writers, 14–17, 58–76
    role of brain in, xiii–xiv, 1
Receptive knowledge, 124
Redd, T., 133, 134
Register, 130
Research paper genre, 121–23
Revising, 39
Rickford, J., 133
Round-robin writing, 13

Sample-predict-confirm process, 5–6
Schemas, 24

Schuster, E. H., 64
Scope creep, 104–7
Scripts, 24
Self-googling, 20–22, 27–28, 110
Semicolons, 54
Sentence gathering, 81–85
Sentences, 77–93
    beginning of, 64–65
    as building blocks, 86–92
    concept and definitions of, 77–81
    length of, 117
    linkages of, 86–92
Series repetition, 18
Short-term memory, 28
Snow, C., xi
Spatt, B., 122
Standard English, misperceptions about,
    130–34
Standard English learners (SELs). See
    Dialectically diverse writers
Students
    dialectically diverse, 126–42
    exposure to writing, 58

Talusan, M., 33
Teaching of writing, strategies for, xii–xiii
Text analysis, 59–68
Thesis statements, 46–48
Titles, reader expectations and, 41–42,
    110–12
Topic-comment relationships, 87–89
Topics, consistency in, 117
Topic sentences, 46–48
Transitions, 14–18, 48–52, 91
    reader expectations and, 48–52
    reconstructing, 14–18, 49–52

Variety, 116–17
Voice, consistency in, 118–19

Walker, A. A., 31
Weaver, C., 136
Webb, K., 133, 134
Willingham, D., 28, 29, 59, 63, 112
Word-for-word reading, 3–5
Word repetition, 117

Writing
    current state of, xi–xii
    deficiencies in, xii

Writing logs, 66–68
Written language, 139

Author

John T. Crow is a professional development consultant. He received his doctorate from the University of Texas in curriculum and instruction, specializing in second language acquisition. His thirty years of classroom experience and interest in human cognition give him a unique perspective on the teaching of composition. He has given workshops all across the United States on the application of brain-based learning to the teaching of writing, focusing on how to take advantage of the mental resources that native and advanced non-native English speakers bring to the classroom. He currently lives in Winter Haven, Florida, with his best friend in all the world (a.k.a. his wife).

This book was typeset in TheMix and Palatino by Barbara Frazier.

The typeface used on the cover is Amadi MT Condensed.

The book was printed on 50-lb. Opaque Offset paper by Versa Press, Inc.